Trump, Trump, Trump

The March of Folly

Also by Susan Ohanian
Recipient of The George Orwell Award
for Distinguished Contribution to Honesty and Clarity in Public Language

Within the Forest: A New Approach to Fairy Tales

Dates with the Greats

Garbage Pizza, Patchwork Quilts, and Math Magic

Who's In Charge? A Teacher Speaks Her Mind

Math as a Way of Knowing

Math at a Glance

Ask Ms. Class

Standards, Plain English, and the Ugly Duckling

One Size Fits Few: The Folly of Educational Standards

Why Is Corporate America Bashing Our Public Schools, with Kathy Emery

Day-By-Day Math

Books Day by Day

The Great Word Catalogue

What Happened to Recess and WHY are Our Children Struggling in Kindergarten?

A Roadblock in Vermont's Design for Education

When Childhood Collides with NCLB

Trump, Trump, Trump
The March of Folly

Susan Ohanian

191 Bank Street
Burlington, Vermont 05401

Copyright © 2019 by Susan Ohanian

Illustrations: Jennifer Cole

All rights reserved. No part of this publication may be reproduced, distributed, or transmitted in any form or by any means, including photocopying, recording, or other electronic or mechanical methods, without the prior written permission of the publisher, except in the case of brief quotations embodied in critical reviews and certain other noncommercial uses permitted by copyright law.

Onion River Press
191 Bank Street
Burlington, VT 05401

ISBN: 978-1-949066-20-3

Library of Congress Control Number: 2019933126

Printed in the United States of America

For the sake of our children, all of them

Contents

I   TRUMPIAD: A Blowhard's Biorama   1

II   TRUMPLOOT: In Midas He Trusts   21

III   TRUMPOTICA: The Women in His Life   31

IV   TRUMPETEERING: The Merchandizing Family   41

V   BEDLAM: Bouncing Along with the Cabinet   53

VI   TRUMPED OUT: Rundown   77

POSTSCRIPT: WHY DID THE DONALD CROSS THE ROAD?   89

I TRUMPIAD:
A Blowhard's Biorama

Newborn in Queens in '46,
And raised with lots of money tricks,
Made his money the old-fashioned way:
Chomping at Dad's business buffet,
Guzzling foul heirloom politics.

His father's middle name was Christ:
Examined for war-profit heists
Made truck with mafia scions.
Ties: what The Donald grew up on.
Surely the family Zeitgeist.

School rules The Donald did defy,
Gave music teacher a black eye.
Trump cites this as showing backbone.
Grade two: "making opinions known"—
Definitely a real tough guy.

Other school behaviors include
More paradigm patterns quite crude.
Making ruckus every-which-way
Was his elementary mainstay,
Early showcase of Trumptitude.

Sent off to military school
For disciplinary re-spool,
He learned aggression diversion; Brags
about finesse incursion—
Ever claiming he holds edge tool.

Fordham tennis and squash first-string.
While making a real-estate fling.
Switched to U of PA in third year,
Where he moved along in low gear— His
eye still on real-estate bling.

Liked to ride 'round New York City
In Mama's Rolls-Royce so pretty.
Claimed at Wharton he had the chops:
Of all the class he was the tops.
School records don't back this ditty.

What you see and hear depends a good deal on where you are standing. It also depends on what sort of person you are.
—C. S. Lewis, *The Chronicles of Narnia: The Magician's Nephew* (1955)

Walker [the teacher Trump punched] heard that Trump was considering a run for the presidency. "When that kid was ten, even then he was a little shit."
—Michael Kranish and Mark Fisher, *Trump Revealed: An American Journey of Ambition, Ego, Money, and Power* (2016)

"He was a brat," said Donald's sister Maryanne Barry. Interview, Feb. 10, 2005—in Timothy L. O'Brien, *TrumpNation: The Art of Being The Donald* (2005)

He was a conniver even then. A real pain in the ass. He would do anything to win.—Ted Tobias, New York Military Academy coach, in Michael D'Antonio, *Never Enough: Donald Trump and the Pursuit of Success* (2015)

[H]e won a medal for "neatness." His roommate…said Trump folded his towels and underwear "so that every single one was perfectly squared—like, insanely neat."
—David Shields, *Nobody Hates Trump More Than Trump: An Intervention* (2018)

He continued helping his father make deals while a student at the Wharton School of Finance at the University of Pennsylvania, from which he graduated first in his class [sic] in 1968. "Donald is the smartest person I know," his father said admiringly.
—Judy Klemesrud, *New York Times*, Nov. 1, 1976

A 1968 commencement program shared by *The Daily Pennsylvanian* shows that Trump graduated from the undergraduate school of finance and commerce, but he did not graduate at the top of his class or with honors.
—Cindy Woodall, *Pennsylvania Real Time News*, Feb. 19, 2017

I'm such a clever Toad.
—Kenneth Grahame, *The Wind in the Willows* (1908)

Liked church of Norman Vincent Peale
With positive-thinking appeal:
"Picturize, prayerize, actualize."
The preacher did duly advise,
Vowing richness to those who kneel.

God embracing business with zeal,
Peale campaigned against the New Deal;
Sound Christians get all due prizes,
In bigger and bigger sizes.
Counselors warned against this spiel.

Bad feet kept Vietnam at bay;
Gained this athlete five draft delays.
On grit, he was scoring zero;
Then smacked McCain "not war hero."
Toxic junk in moral melee.

On radio without a qualm
Said dating was like Vietnam.
Smashing all ethical guidelines:
 "Vaginas potential landmines,"
All uttered with pride and aplomb.

A windbag looking for notice,
Ever feeding on detritus.
With the gall of Pinocchio,
Throwing out braggadocio,
All for want of ego poultice.

Personal doc gave glowing score:
"Astonishing health" came the roar.
Press noted similarities
To Trump's word peculiarities
In Doc's show of esprit de corps.

In office, Trump has grown an inch:
Such increase for most not a cinch.
Tagged as overweight, not obese.
So now health concerns can surcease
And quarter pounders he can clinch.

Peale gave ardent opposition to FDR and the New Deal.
—David Brody & Scott Lamp, *The Faith of Donald J. Trump: A Spiritual Biography* (2018)

Reverend Peale was the type of minister that I liked and I liked him personally... I especially loved his sermons.
—Donald Trump, *Good Again: How to Fix Our Crippled America* [formerly titled *Crippled America*] (2015)

Trump seemed the picture of health…played football, tennis and squash…But after he graduated from college… making him eligible to be drafted and sent to Vietnam, he received a diagnosis… bone spurs in his heels [resulting] in a coveted 1-Y medical deferment…—Steve Eder & Dave Philipps, *New York Times*, Aug. 1, 2016

[A] possible explanation…involves a foot doctor in Queens who rented his office from Mr. Trump's father, Fred C. Trump, and a suggestion that the diagnosis was granted as a courtesy to the elder Mr. Trump.—Steve Eder, *New York Times*, Dec. 26, 2018

Conscientious objectors deserve a huge amount of credit for taking a principled stand."—Robert Mueller, Special Counsel for U.S. Department of Justice, Marine in Quant Tri: Bronze Star, two Navy commendation medals, the Purple Heart, and the Vietnamese Cross of Gallantry, to Cullen Couch, *UVA Lawyer*, Fall 2002

"[I]t is a dangerous world out there…my personal Vietnam. I feel like a great and very brave soldier," Trump said…when Howard Stern asked him how he handled making sure he wasn't contracting STDs from the women he was sleeping with…[Trump] called women's vaginas "potential landmines," saying, "there's some real danger there."
—Ale Russian, *People,* Oct. 28, 2016

Ronny L. Jackson, the veterans affairs nominee…gave Trump an excellent bill of health, including a declaration that the president, while overweight, is just shy of being officially obese—thanks to having apparently grown an inch in office.—Paul Krugman, *New York Times*, March 30, 2018
Note: Adults begin to shrink by a quarter to a third of an inch every decade after age 40, thanks to changes in our bones, muscles and joints.—AARP Health Living blog, Sept 21, 2011.

Trumpancy

Close at hand inside the stable
Roy Cohn there, Trump to enable:
Formulating bias lawsuits.
Narrowing the prenup breadfruit.
Fixing cement crews timetables.

In transactions not Capraesque,
Marched in tune with the Kafkaesque
So that contractors stayed in line,
Following just what he assigned,
Photo of Cohn on office desk.

With the polish of a porker,
Trump offered huge creepy corkers.
Starred in debut issue of Spy,
Whose conclusion none did belie:
"One of 10 Most Embarrassing NYers."

Spy ranked people on a "Trump-score,"
How they were like Trump at the core,
The "short-fingered vulgarian"
Who in his wake left carrion.
They itemized globs to abhor.

A face the color of Cheetos;
Pride buzz worse than mosquitoes.
The makeup from Benjamin-Moore
Impossible to account for:
Orange staging: Fritos/Doritos.

Ring-a-ding-a-ling-ding-ding-ding!
We have Agent Orange in West Wing.
With attention span of seconds,
Disrupted when Twitter beckons
With messages all molesting.

Then New York's most feared lawyer, Mr. Cohn had a client list that ran the gamut from the disreputable to the quasi-reputable: Anthony (Fat Tony) Salerno, Claus von Bulow, George Steinbrenner. But there was one client who occupied a special place in Roy Cohn's famously cold heart: Donald J. Trump.—Jonathan Mahler & Matt Flegenheimer, *New York Times*, June 20, 2016

Cohn was by the early seventies a walking advertisement for every form of graft, the best-known fixer in New York… [When Cohn was dying of AIDS] Donald quickly began withdrawing work… "I can't believe he's doing this to me," Roy complained. "Donald pisses ice water."—Wayne Barrett, *Trump: The Greatest Show on Earth* (1992)

My fingers are long and beautiful as, it has been well documented, are various other parts of my body.
—Donald Trump to Maureen Callahan, *New York Post*, April 3, 2011

"[Marco Rubio] referred to my hands, if they're small, something else must be small. I guarantee you there's no problem. I guarantee it."
—Donald Trump, GOP debate, March 3, 2016

The worst thing a man can do is go bald," Trump warned one of his top executives. "Never let yourself go bald."
—Harry Hurt III, *Lost Tycoon: The Many Lives of Donald J. Trump* (1993)

He strokes his flying fuzz-mane. It looks gorgeous, like it's been recently fed.
—Matt Taibbi, *Rolling Stone*, Feb. 24, 2016

[Caesar] The Dandy whom Cicero once refused to take seriously because he paid too much attention to his hairstyle.
—Barry Strauss, *The Death of Caesar* (2015)

Yes, laugh when a president's tie
Is scotch-taped in fashion awry.
Front side is not sartorial
Backside needing tutorial
But this, of course, is such small fry.

On the Trump speech Inaugural
George W. Bush the goods did spill:
Observing, "That was some weird shit."
The speech vainglorious befits—
Would it had been exaugural.

A man who's never diffident:
He claims himself Magnificent.
Firing cabinet with Tweet sound bites,
Assures his media limelight.
Congress must end Omnipotence!

Using self as main consultant
With hot-potato resultant.
Brags about his "very good brain."
Oh, Mary Jane, Mary Jane Jane.
It's so much worse than repugnant.

But even a White House cuckoo
Sees one Twitter topic taboo.
He insults all who annoy him,
But Stormy's name crushes his vim.
Shoo, Storm. Shoo! Shoo! Shoo!

Give nod for media handling:
Behavior sparks front page
branding. Loud candidacy cotillion
Pushed those free ads worth $5 billion.
Media manna ace landing.

Whether its kudos or abuse,
For Trump all press news is good news.
As media notes this mucker,
We have to ask: Who's the sucker
When he gets big payoff transfuse?

Trump suggested a tip from his own wardrobe to Chris Christie: To make yourself look thinner, wear a long tie.
—Matt Stieb, *New York* Intelligencer, Jan 16, 2019

The guy is still (still!) taping his damn tie together.
—Scott Christian, *Esquire*, Jan. 20, 2017

This is a great day for me personally. You're very smart to have voted for me…I don't know how much the government paid for the Washington Monument—and I have no problem with George Washington, but he wasn't a businessman—they overpaid. You've got a 560-foot tall structure sitting on some of the most prime real estate in the country.—Christopher Buckley, "The Donald Goes to Washington," *Wall Street Journal*, Oct 21, 1999

With just 10 days before he finishes his first year as president, Trump has made 2,001 false or misleading claims in 355 days, according to our data base that analyzes, categorizes and tracks every suspect statement uttered by the president. That's an average of more than 5.6 claims a day.—Glenn Kessler & Meg Kelly, *Washington Post*, Jan. 10, 2018

Trump's tsunami of untruths helped push the count in The Fact Checker's database past 5,000 on the 601st day of his presidency.
—Glenn Kessler, Salvador Rizzo, & Meg Kelly, *Washington Post*, Sept. 13, 2018

It's amazing how often I am right, only to be criticized by the media. Illegal immigration, take the oil, build the wall, Muslims, NATO!
—@realDonaldTrump, Twitter, March 23, 2016

The verbose commander in chief has posted more than 2,900 times on Twitter since taking office, using the term "FAKE NEWS" to describe everything from the Russia inquiry and allegations of chaos in the White House to harassment accusations, the size of his inaugural crowds and heated arguments with world leaders…But he has been uncharacteristically silent in recent days—to the relief of his advisers—as pornographic film star and a Playboy model shared intimate details of sexual encounters with Mr. Trump.
—Michael D. Shear & Maggie Haberman, *New York Times*, March 26, 2018

Trumpenaeum

Lots of books do carry Trump's name
In what amounts to a shell game.
Other people hired as the scribes,
The Donald ethos to describe.
Then he brags about the books' fame.

With a flock of ghosts in his thrall,
Some doubt that Donald writes at all.
Yes, he does tweet and tweet and tweet.
But that's quite a freakish drumbeat—
An onslaught of verbal paintballs,

There's a lot of chitter-chatter
On who's that account's mad hatter.
Scavino, at media job,
Is known for vicious Trump tweet lobs.
Trump in headlines is what matters.

Trump's a famed author without pen,
As highbrow as a guinea hen.
Twitter requires no lofty mien,
Easy format that lets Trump preen,
Press does feature ever again.

Tony Schwartz wrote *Art of the Deal*,
Showing Donald as the big wheel.
Later when talking of this gig,
Schwartz admits: "Put lipstick on a pig."
The tycoon was really a heel.

But what matters is the heyday,
Giving Trump the right to sashay.
Fifty-one weeks on the *Times* list;
Trump with bang-up acclaim was kissed.
A total media payday.

Schwartz suggests a reframe,
Giving the book wildly new name.
He'd call it *The Sociopath*,
Belladonna in primrose swath
Winding round Trump's chronic con game.

I'm very highly educated. I know words. I know the best words.
—Donald J. Trump, campaign event, South Carolina, Dec. 30, 2015

Dan Scavino, the president's former golf caddy, now oversees the White House's messaging on social media. Scavino is in many ways the president's mini-me, a man whose bombast, impulse control and instinct for a good punch match those of his boss.
—Eliana Johnson, *Politico*, June 10, 2017

So I wrote a book called *The Art of the Deal*, which as you know, is the biggest of all time.
—Donald Trump to Timothy L. O'Brien: *TrumpNation, The Art of Being The Donald* (2005)

The president has long sold himself as a self-made billionaire, but a *Times* investigation found that he received at least $413 million in today's dollars from his father's real estate empire, much of it through tax dodges in the 1990s.
—David Barstow, Susanne Craig, & Russ Buettner, *New York Times*, Oct. 2, 2018

Caligula had the heads knocked off the statues of the other gods and replaced with his own image.
—Farquhar, Michael, *A Treasure of Royal Scandals* (2001)

The only people who get famous on their own are serial killers.
—Nathan Hill, *The Nix* (2016)

Leggy beaut on *The Post's* Page Six
Did become The Donald's ghost pick
For *Trump: The Art of the Comeback.*
Filled with Donald ego jam-packed,
It is a self-service speedy fix.

Then *Trump: Think Like a Billionaire*
Does numerous Trump judgments blare:
From best credit card, best shampoo,
To the best Broadway show run-through.
Nothing on which he won't declare.

Advises, "You are what you eat,"
Mar-a-Lago feed can't be beat.
Visit the Mar-a-Lago Club
For insider dope on great grub.
Advice from The Donald's front seat.

Considering self royalty,
The Donald demands loyalty
In rite of corporate hardball.
"I'm screwing them against the wall!"
He verbalizes joyfully.

When Trump asked what he was reading,
The viewers saw mental bleeding.
Said, "I'm trying to get started."
Then his sophistry departed:
He needed a cue-card feeding.

Reading. "I'm looking at a book…"
Then he bolted from grappling hook:
"A lot of great things happening…
Lots of tremendous things happening."
Rather talk of pocketbook.

He could have mentioned his letter
To *New York Times*, a go-getter.
Praising self, he trashed two authors,
Claiming they were just big rotters;
He was best selling go-getter.

[*Trump: The Art of the Comeback* is] a serenade to self, cut into chapters," a book that "requires a lot of the reader—mainly the patience to endure the domineering ego, the boorish asides, the self-serving pronouncements.
—Fred Andrews, *New York Times*, Dec. 13, 1997

Trump called Kate Bohner, the ghostwriter of *Trump: The Art of the Comeback,* "Katsey-Watsey."—Candace Bushnell, *The Observer*, Nov 1, 1997

A few years earlier, Bohner, a University of Pennsylvania grad, appeared in a full-page *New York Times* hosiery ad clad in a black slip and spiked heels.
 —Emily Peck, Huffington Post, April 13, 2017

After a series of scandals and affairs, real and imagined, Bohner left the firm [Lazare Freeres]. After several career cycles, she is currently a Buddhist nun, has a YouTube channel…—Irin Carmon, Jezebel, April 2, 2010

On Trump Force One there were four major food groups: McDonald's, Kentucky Fried Chicken, pizza and Diet Coke… Trump's team flew on junk food. —Corey Lewandowski & David N. Bossie, *Let Trump Be Trump: The Inside Story of His Rise to the Presidency* (2017)

During the bad times, I learned who was loyal and who wasn't. I believe in an eye for an eye. A couple of people who betrayed me need my help now, and I am screwing them against the wall!
—Donald J. Trump, *Trump: The Art of the Comeback* (1997)

Fox host Tucker Carlson: What do you do at the end of the day? What do you read, what do you watch?"

Trump: Well, you know, I love to read. Actually, I'm looking at a book, I'm reading a book, I'm trying to get started
 —Madeleine Sheehan Perkins, *Business Insider*, March 16, 2017

I've read John Updike. I've read Orham Pamuk, I've read Philip Roth…Mark Singer was not born with great writing ability…writing about remarkable people who are clearly outside of his realm. I've been a best-selling author for close to 20 years.
—Donald Trump, letter, *New York Times*, Sept. 11, 2005

Wonder who wrote that epistle,
Filled with literary gristle
To applaud The Great Donald Show.
Who's it penned by? Nobody knows—
But signed as Trumpian missal.

Now high the roofbeams we must raise:
For Judith Krantz, Trump had big praise,
She set novel in Trump Tower
Showing Donald in full flower.
One more bit of Trump ego graze.

It matters not Krantz book was panned.
The Donald was just the straight man,
He got sought-after coherences
And some TV appearances,
Well fitting his attention span.

Didn't read book by O'Brien,
But chose to sue him for lyin'.
Some aides had offered facts to swear
That Trump wasn't a billionaire.
Judge dismissal left Trump cryin'.

He's intuitive, Trump declares.
Then does explain with his great flare,
"I read areas... passages."
Call him the king of savages,
A swellhead loving Fox News fare.

We've increased vocabulary.
He's given us words to parry:
"Carnage," "emoluments," "recuse"
Make us sing the Impeachment blues.
"Dotard" called up dictionary.

Reading drove Madame Bovary:
Adultery, debt, end sorry.
Dumpenführer is right on cue
With the steps number one and two.
Surely rat poison is past due.

Donald Trump, the brilliant, ambitious young real-estate man whom even his enemies had to admit was disarmingly unaffected…Maxi looked for Donald Trump's damp pocket handkerchief, for he carried nothing as common as a Kleenex.—Judith Krantz, *I'll Take Manhattan* (1986)

[Krantz's] new novel…follows the formula she devised for "Scruples," "Princess Daisy" and "Mistral's Daughter'—lots of rich people, lots of designer clothes and a measured amount of brisk, clinical sex…One hesitates…to come down very hard on a book with no more literary aspirations than a box of Froot Loops.
—Laura Shapiro, *New York Times*, May 4, 1986

I didn't read [*TrumpNation: The Art of Being The Donald*, by Timothy L. O'Brien], to be honest with you…I never read it. I saw some of the things they said…I said, 'Go sue him. It will cost him a lot of money.'
—Donald Trump to David A. Fahrenthold & Robert O'Harrow Jr., *Washington Post*, Aug. 10, 2016

[Twenty-four years after] Harry Hurt III published a biography of Donald Trump, Trump had security guards escort Hurt's group, which included billionaire David Koch—a prominent Republican donor and member of the Trump International Golf Club in West Palm Beach—off the premises.—Sam Dangremond, *Town & Country*, Jan. 4, 2017

Don't believe the crap you see from these people, the fake news…What you're seeing and what you're reading is not what's happening.—Donald Trump, speech, annual convention, VFW, July 24, 2018

Responding directly for the first time to President Trump's threat at the United Nations to destroy nuclear-armed North Korea, its leader called Mr. Trump a "mentally deranged U.S. dotard."
—Choe Sang-Hun, *New York Times*, Sept. 22, 2017

The more you read, the more things you'll know.
The more that you learn, the more places you'll go.
   —Dr. Suess, *I Can Read with My Eyes Shut!* (1978)

Trumpalooza

The Donald hired feng shui master
To look at tower pilasters.
But recall: he is only awed
When the bankers loudly applaud
And hand him financing faster.

Architect urged on letter size:
Smaller would styling optimize.
For Trump, bigger is far better:
He went for twice-as-large letters,
For his name to capitalize.

Trump Tower at 56th Street
Is far far far far from discreet.
Trump's priapic temple to self
Is well-stacked off top-money shelf,
With gold elevators complete.

In staggering self-portraiture,
Trump claims he's aesthete by nature.
With The Donald's swelled submissions,
It's all in the definition.
He defines the nomenclature.

Of polysyllables he's shy:
Favorite words are "Me" and "I."
Trump's elocutionary style
Does make George W. Bush erstwhile
Sound like Nabokov on the fly.

Claims to be in things top drawer;
Anything you name, he knows more.
Ever-constant with self-applause,
Listing his greatness, there's no pause.
But as in golf, he's keeping score.

In grandeur, nothing's too weighty.
"No one reads Bible more than me."
Bible to bullets, no mute swan,
Always declares top echelon:
"I authorize my military."

[Feng shui] is just another element in which you can have the advantage over your competitors. Asians are becoming a big part of our market and this is something we can't ignore.
—Donald Trump in Ashley Dunn, *New York Times*, Sept. 22, 1994

Architect Der Scutt argued that "the height of the Trump Tower letters would be more elegant if they were only eighteen inches high." Trump intercepted the shop drawing…and changed the design…to thirty-six-inches.
—Wayne Barrett, *Trump: The Greatest Show on Earth* (1992)

I think I am, actually humble.—Donald Trump, "60 Minutes" interview, July 17, 2016

I realized early on that I was an aesthete by nature, being attracted to beauty in both people and buildings. My work has shown that some early self-knowledge was right on target.
—Donald Trump & Meredith McIver, *Trump: How to Get Rich* (2004)

He was the king of hyperbole and he had just the requisite touch of Elvis vulgarity to endear him to the common man.
—Liz Smith, *Natural Blonde: A Memoir* (2000)

[Y]ou might as well tell people how great you are because nobody else is going to do it.
—Donald Trump in Timothy L. O'Brien, *TrumpNation: The Art of Being The Donald* (2005)

In his current dread of polysyllables…he makes George W. Bush sound like Vladimir Nabokov…[T]ranscripts of his speaking appearances often look like complete gibberish.
—Matt Taibbi, *Rolling Stone*, Sept. 19, 2017

The American electoral system is opening before him like a flower…[T]his boorish, monosyllabic TV tyrant with the attention span of an Xbox-playing 11-year-old really is set to lay waste to the most impenetrable oligarchy the Western world ever devised.
—Matt Taibbi, *Rolling Stone*, Feb. 24, 2016

I alone can fix it.—Donald Trump, Republican National Convention, July 21, 2016

The Donald tweets: In a crisis
"I know more than generals about ISIS."
"I understand things. Believe me."
In onslaught of verbal debris,
We feel we're in cytolisis.

He is for torture resorting:
"Hell of a lot worse than waterboarding."
But don't fret; says he can revise,
If ever wrong, he'll apologize.
Let's just hope there's recording.

Please hammer loudly the drumbeat:
Humble Donald defines elite.
"Bigger, more beautiful apartment,"
Also has White House compartment.
Gilting Yuge, his conceit complete.

With golden toilet within reach.
A White House can be in Palm Beach.
And a matter incidental:
We pay big for golf cart rental
To clubs owned by White House leech.

The Donald does explain ego—
But not quite in terms loligo.
Ego is needed for success.
Jesus and Teresa: full dress.
Thus we get the Trump testigo.

His likeness won't go on Rushmore,
But here's a plan for Trump-de-corps.
Trump self-promotion gadgetry
Could heed Kim Jung-Un badgetry:
Citizens wear proof of ardor.

Caps, T-shirts, bracelets, tattoos—
All offering The Donald muse:
The Donald Makes Us Great Again!
Amen. Amen. Amen. Amen.
Gains with piety: Great Trump ooze.

What I do is I authorize my military," Trump told a press pool…after senior U.S. commanders in Afghanistan decided to drop the largest conventional [non-nuclear] ammunition since World War II.
—John T. Bennett, *Roll Call*, May 11, 2017

You should be killing guys. You don't need a strategy to kill people.—Donald Trump on Afghanistan, in Bob Woodward: *Fear: Trump in the White House* (2018)

I'm also honored to have the greatest temperament that anybody has…the temperament of knowing how to win.
—Donald Trump, Florida rally, Nov. 3, 2016

I win, I win, I always win. In the end I always win, whether it's in golf, whether it's in tennis, whether it's in life. I just always win. And I tell people I always win, because I do.
—Donald Trump in Timothy L. O'Brien, *TrumpNation: The Art of Being The Donald* (2005)

[Caligula] had the heads knocked off the statues of the other gods and replaced with his own image.—Michael Farquhar, *The Treasury of Royal Scandals* (2001)

I think apologizing's a great thing, but you have to be wrong. I will absolutely apologize, sometime in the hopefully distant future, if I'm ever wrong.—Donald Trump, "The Tonight Show," Sept. 11, 2015

The Secret Service has spent at least $137,595 to rent golf carts to protect President Trump this year at his private clubs in New Jersey and Florida.
—Julia Fair, *USA Today*, Oct. 5, 2017

DT: Every successful person has a very large ego.
Playboy: Mother Teresa? Jesus Christ?
DT: Far greater egos than you will ever understand. [O]ur country needs more ego. —*Playboy*, March 1990

Members of the United Nations General Assembly laughed at Donald Trump after he told them his administration had "accomplished more than almost any ... in the history of our country."
—Clark Mindock, *The Independent*, Sept. 25, 2018

[North Korean[Citizens over the age of sixteen are expected to wear a badge celebrating at least one of the Kims.—Evan Osnos, *The New Yorker*, Sept. 18, 2017

Now pay close attention to this:
Bannon quashed cerebral abyss.
Digging deep for explanation,
Gives proto-mystic causation:
Granting head version of the cuisse.

He said Trump gets stereotypes
From pondering Jung's archetypes.
Book for which he has affection
Is *Memory, Dreams, Reflections*.
This must get us hunting for snipe.

Christians should now stand by, assured:
Mike Pence has sent the hallowed word.
Announcing with great clarity,
Trump has highest integrity.
Whew! Public confidence secured.

Trump insists he's no church slacker:
At times, he gets "little cracker."
He says, "Nothing beats the Bible...
Not even *Art of the Deal* rivals."
On religion, he's a yacker.

Trump finds Bible "incredible":
In each part, this book's sellable.
Praise for testaments Old and New,
Reciting a verse he won't do.
But it's the book phenomenal.

Donald's religion is spotty,
And sometimes even quite dotty.
Comfy with condominiums,
He referenced "Two Corinthians,"
And a Proverbs quote chapatti.

On Ayn Rand, he's more specific:
Howard Roark is quite terrific.
But even that is only bluff,
Appearing like *Cliff Notes* cream puff.
Useful as audience gimmick.

Although the mainstream media and other haters give him little credit for his intellect, Donald Trump has more than a fundamental grasp on a surprising number of fields, including Jungian psychology. One of his favorite books is *Memory, Dreams, Reflections*, Jung's autobiography.
—Corey Lewandowski & David N. Bossie, *Let Trump Be Trump: The Inside Story of His Rise to the Presidency* (2017)

Question: You mention the Bible—you've been talking about how it's your favorite book…I'm wondering what one or two of your most favorite Bible verses are and why.
Trump: I—wouldn't wanna get into it, because to me that's very personal…I don't wanna get into verses.
—John Heilemann & Mark Halperin, Bloomberg Politics, Aug. 26, 2015

Character matters to the presidency and Donald Trump will bring the highest level of integrity to the highest office in the land. You can count on it.—Mike Pence, Living Word Bible Church, Mesa, AZ, Sept. 22, 2016

Ivana Trump told her lawyer that from time to time her husband reads a book of Hitler's collected speeches, *My New Order*, which he keeps in a cabinet by his bed.
—Marie Brenner, *Vanity Fair*, Sept. 1990

He's exactly the sort of person who would want you to think he's an Ayn Rand fan, while he really acts like one of her villains.
—Robert Tracinski, *The Federalist*, April 22, 2016

Trump described himself as an Ayn Rand fan. He said of her novel *The Fountainhead*, "It relates to business (and) beauty (and) life and inner emotions." He identified with Howard Roark, the novel's idealistic protagonist who designs skyscrapers and rages against the establishment.
—Kirsten Powers, *USA Today*, April 11, 2017

Until and unless you discover that money is the root of all good, you ask for your own destruction.
—Ayn Rand, *Atlas Shrugged* (1957)

If, with the Adolf and Ayn Rand,
Trump plods in a moral quicksand,
He finds a new book to commend:
Evangelical recommend
For Robert Jeffress, his big fan.

Bashing Muslims, Catholics, Gays,
Here's someone giving great praise.
The two show shared admiration,
Giving pat-on-back citations.
A twin agenda they do blaze.

Pastor Jeffress quotes the Bible
In ways to suit Trump so primal:
Build a wall;
Send a nuclear squall;
These acts are all in God's vital.

Doctrinists in constant prayer
Just for Hillary to forswear.
Choosing Donald as God's proxy
To bring back their orthodoxy
And to be the evil slayer.

Trump's win is seen as God's design;
Evangelicals there in line
To celebrate their victory.
They see God's benedictory
Safekeeping their values enshrined.

Long planning brought Trump's gyration
Prepping for faith jubilation.
Called faith leaders to Trump Tower
To bask in their fervent shower,
While Demos mired in cunctation.

A savvy influence seeder,
He talked-the-talks with faith leaders,
Went to Billy Graham birthday bash,
Pulling in his religious cache
Sending out faith-filled feeders.

"I really believe the Lord is speaking to me, and maybe I'm supposed to run for President.—Donald Trump to Paula White, controversial Pentecostal evangelist, in 2012, in David Brody & Scott Lamb, *The Faith of Donald J. Trump: A Spiritual Biography* (2018)

Great book just out. "A Place called Heaven" by Dr. Robert Jeffress—A wonderful man!
—@realDonaldTrump, Twitter, Oct. 20, 2017

[Citing Romans 13], Texas megachurch pastor Robert Jeffress, one of President Trump's evangelical advisers who preached the morning of his inauguration, has released a statement saying the president has the moral [Biblical] authority to do whatever, whether it's assassination, capital punishment or evil punishment, to quell the actions of evildoers like Kim Jong Un.
—Sarah Pulliam Bailey, *Washington Post*, Aug. 9, 2017

We had a new president, one we believed God had raised up for such a time as this. And perhaps best of all, we each thanked God in our own way that Hillary Clinton was not going to be the next commander-in-chief.
—Stephen E. Strang, *God and Donald Trump* (2017)

"It is God that raises up a king," according to Paula White, a prosperity gospel preacher who has advised Mr. Trump.
—Katherine Stewart, *New York Times*, Dec. 31, 2018

The victory of Donald Trump with 81 percent of the evangelical vote…—Frances Fitzgerald, *The Evangelicals: The Struggle to Shape America* (2017)

He met with evangelical leaders to reassure them that he would still pursue their agenda…The Christians know all the things I'm doing for them, right?" he asked.
—Maggie Haberman, Glenn Thrush & Peter Baker, *New York Times*, Dec. 9, 2017

Evangelist Franklin Graham said that Christians shouldn't necessarily be concerned by Donald Trump's troubling history, because the GOP presidential candidate was one of "many people" who "gave their hearts to Christ" at his father Billy Graham's 95th birthday party in 2013.
—Miranda Blue, Right Wing Watch, Nov. 8, 2016

For interview with CBN
Trump displayed his quite savvy ken
In setting a pious tempo.
Out came confirmation photo,
With voice of pride. Amen. Amen.

Of course Hillary went missing
From such Bible brigade kissing.
And she found it too boreable
To speak to the deplorables.
Voters lost in Heartland dissing.

Endlessly when he jaws and jaws,
He calls on God's pragmatic laws.
He's a charismatic magnet,
Building a Christian cabinet.
Applause. Applause. Applause, Applause.

Yes, it was an obstacle race
To undercut the Trump embrace.
The Faithful spurn as pettifog
The conduct of the wretched dog,
Because their God put him in place.

We'll long suffer the brutal bloat
Of the evangelical vote.
The steadfast faithful won't leave him.
No matter his behavior grim—
Trump's safe behind megachurch moat.

Trumposis

Brags about how little he sleeps:
"I toss, I turn, I beep-de-beep,
I want to know what's going on."
So out go those Tweets before dawn.
We wish he would try counting sheep.

After barbed GOP debate,
Trump went on a manic Tweet-Spate:
Between two and four thirty a.m.
Thirty crappy burst from Trump phlegm.
Needed: Someone to call checkmate.

The Brody File spoke exclusively with Trump at Trump Tower…Lots of interesting answers about issues important to Evangelicals.—David Brody, CBN [Christian Broadcasting Network], April 8, 2011

Republican nominee Donald Trump said the United States has "lost a true patriot" as he spoke at the funeral of Phyllis Schafly.. "Phyllis was there for me when it was not at all fashionable.—Rebecca Morin, *Politico*, Sept. 16, 2016

"He wasn't asking for an endorsement or a contribution. He was looking to hear the heartbeat of the faith community."
—evangelical minister Paula White, in R. Sands, *The Washington Times*, Oct. 11, 2018

[Y]ou could put half of Trump's supporters into what I call the basket of deplorables. Right? The racist, sexist, homophobic, xenophobic, Islamaphobic…And he has lifted them up.
—Hillary Clinton, New York fundraiser, Sept. 9, 2016

As president of the United States, Donald Trump has been put in a position of authority by Almighty God.
 —David Brody & Scott Lamb, *The Faith of Donald J. Trump: A Spiritual Biography* (2018)

[The annual prayer breakfast] has become an international influence-peddling bazaar, where foreign dignitaries, religious leaders, diplomats and lobbyists jockey for access to the highest reaches of American power.—Kenneth P. Vogel and Elizabeth Dias, *New York Times*, July 27, 2018

He's a great believer in his almost sadomasochistic practice of enforced insomnia. He thinks it is one of the secrets behind his stunning success. —Harry Hurt III, *Lost Tycoon: The Many Lives of Donald J. Trump*, (1993)

It's possible that Trump's biggest problem is that he hasn't slept since 1997…Maybe all the man needs is a good nap.
 —Joy Behar, *The Great Gasbag: An A to Z Study Guide to Surviving Trump World* (2017)

Hypomaniacs are whirlwinds of activity who are filled with energy and need little sleep… They are restless, impatient and easily bored, needing constant stimulation.
—John D. Gartner, Ph.D., clinical psychologist, in *The Dangerous Case of Donald Trump: 27 Psychiatrists and Mental Health Experts Assess a President* (2017)

Covfefe brought us late night mess
To amuse "the negative press."
The entire message stopped right there;
Offering nothing more to share—
Just an ideation abscess.

Trump acutely liked to hob-nob
On first 100 days on the job.
He said it went super okay,
And promptly gave himself an A,
While sensible folk sat and sobbed.

After ten days, we felt exhaust
From the unstoppable accost:
Tweet fatigue and alternate facts.
Congress needs to give him the axe.
Trumpdom comes at too high a cost.

Standing before a Phoenix throng,
The Donald sang his ugly song:
Longer than an hour loon-a-thon.
Presidential sine qua non:
Raging invective ding-ding-dong.

Loudly squawking ten lies a day
Keeps any real world blues away.
For him, lying is essential,
Making him feel consequential:
Deceit is his ego squeeze play.

PolitiFact.com rates 69% of orations
In major need of deflations.
Sort of False, False-y, "Pants on Fire."
Offering a phony esquire
Absent of verification.

And *The New York Times* citation
Offers more documentation:
Twenty-five lies on first 40 days;
We sit and wait for *Congress* blaze.
Nation needs White House ablation.

Despite the constant negative press covfefe
—@realDonaldTrump, Twitter, 5/3/17, 12:06 a.m.

[W]hen Trump returned to Washington from Mar-a-Lago, he set a White House record with a sixteen-tweet day. He behaved less like a President than like a teen-ager locked in his room with an ounce of Purple Skunk, three Happy Meals, and a cell phone.
—David Remnick, *The New Yorker*, Jan 14, 2018

So the next time you consider sending that late-night Tweet or (hopefully not) work-related email, don't succumb to "Trump Syndrome."
—Daniel Barron, resident psychiatrist at Yale University, *Scientific American*, Oct. 17, 2016

[Phoenix]: Seventy-seven minutes of dog whistles… sounding more like a segregationist throwback than an American president.
—Mattathias Schwartz, *GQ*, Nov. 20, 2017

I just find [Trump's Phoenix remarks] extremely disturbing. I really question his ability to be—his fitness to be—in this office, and I also am beginning to wonder about his motivation for it.
—James Clapper, former director of national intelligence, CNN, Aug. 24, 2017

We have catalogued nearly every outright lie he has told publicly since taking the oath of office.
—David Leonhardt & Stuart A. Thompson, *New York Times*, June 23, 2017

[S]ome people said it was the single best speech ever made in that chamber.—Donald J. Trump of his first speech to joint session of Congress, April 24, 2017

Non-partisan fact checkers at PolitiFact concluded that after examining hundreds of Trump's statements, just 15 percent could be classified as "mostly true" or "true."
—Anthony Dimaggio, *CounterPunch*, June 12, 2016

[Gary] Cohn realized again what he had said before to others about the president: "He's a professional liar."
—Bob Woodward, *Fear: Trump in the White House* (2018)

Hedge funds meet at Mar-a-Lago
Schmoozing with White House imago.
If North Korea fires missile,
For sure, the Trumpster will whistle
And Tweet-Tweet with much farrago.

But chocolate cake can't be beat;
Xi Jinping found it quite a treat
During slap-down on Syria.
Yes, a Trumpian valkyrie
To show who's in the chichi seat.

Armed-force missiles during a meal
With China's leader shows Trump zeal.
Really, there can be no mistake:
There's nothing like chocolate cake
For mind extracorporeal.

Trump is also fond of Big Macs,
Oreos in really big stacks,
And KFC by the bucket.
A vegetable? He will duck it.
And Lays chips? Just truck in the sacks.

Two Big Macs, two Filet-of-Fish
Said to be a lunchtime delish—
Along with a chocolate shake.
For dinner it's over-done steak
And cherry vanilla is wish.

Once refused a Japanese dish:
"Not going to eat any fucking raw fish."
Better at McDonald's Japanese;
Taste buds there easy to appease
With his frontrunner foodie swish.

Seated at China state dinner
Trump almost came up a winner.
Supplementing Chicken Kung Pao:
Stewed steak in tomato sauce chow.
Not finger lickin', but no sinner.

President Trump was enjoying the "most beautiful piece of chocolate cake that you've ever seen" when he ordered the air strike on a Syrian airfield last week. Moments later he told Chinese president Xi Jinping—who was digging into some cake of his own—about the strike. —Adam K. Raymond, Daily Intelligencer, April 12, 2017

[The three-layered cake] the Trump chocolate cake (like everything he sells, it has TRUMP embossed on it).
—Helena Horton, *The Telegraph*, April 13, 2017

"There's nothing more American and more of-the-people than fast food," said Ross Schriefer, a Republican strategist and ad maker. "It is the peculiarity of the brand that he's able to be on his multimillion-dollar jet with the gold and black branding and colors, and at the same time eat KFC."
—Ashley Parker, *New York Times*, Aug. 8, 2016

Some of you may have seen the commercial I did for McDonald's. I didn't have to act—I like McDonald's and am a loyal customer.—Donald Trump & Meredith McIver, *Trump: How to Get Rich* (2004)

"I'm not going to eat any fucking raw fish…" Before [the formal dinner with bankers] is served, Donald gets up and walks out, leaving his underlings to deal with their insulted hosts.—Harry Hurt III, *Lost Tycoon: The Many Lives of Donald J. Trump*, (1993)

He has always relished gossiping over plates of well-done steak, salad slathered with Roquefort dressing and bacon crumbles, tureens of gravy and huge slices of dessert with extra ice cream…He also drinks a dozen Diet Cokes a day.
—Maggie Haberman, Glenn Thrush, & Peter Baker,
New York Times, Dec. 9, 2017

With media, the Tweet-in-Chief
Taps a Nixon/Hoffa motif,
Refers to self: "The President."
Feet free; only mind's in cement,
Boosting self as ruler of fief.

Leaving prudence to be tabled,
Scrapped rule on the psych disabled.
Claiming they can take care of selves,
His new rules put guns on their shelves.
We must ask just who's unstable.

Trump did mark his ninety-ninth day
Telling the NRA array,
Yes! Yes! You did come through for me,
And now you will surely agree
I am now here for you. Hooray!

Trump boosters include Charlie Sheen,
And also Jon Voight's shining beam.
There's Kanye West and Stacy Dash
Grabbing insight out of the trash,
Squatting in the show biz ravine.

Trump tributes should worry bestir;
He urged vote for child molester.
Let him cheer Lolita Express,
But please get us out of this mess.
The Donald needs a sequester.

Blast at Gold-Star parents whacko,
Showing insight of a taco.
To quash grieving parents' crises,
Trump blares his own sacrifices,
Ego out-front maniaco.

For him, a bang-up sacrifice
Is buying marble and not gneiss.
Asked to name sacrificial act,
Trump can't speak or make eye contact.
He knows only the asking price.

Nixon was in the habit of referring to himself in the third person, something I had never heard anyone do before—not even members of the Royal Family.
—Michael Korda, *The New Yorker*, May 9, 1993

[I]n an interview with *The New York Times*, Trump recently referred to himself as 'the president'—Jimmy Hoffa style, employing the third-person singular.
—Ramona Naddaff, *Washington Spectator*, Sept. 12, 2017

China has total respect for Donald Trump and Donald Trump's very, very large brain.—Donald Trump, news conference at United Nations, Sept. 27, 2018

Rachel Maddow points out the irony of Donald Trump's remarks that the Las Vegas shooter was "sick and demented" when one of Trump's only legislative accomplishments was a law to make it easier for the mentally ill to get guns.
—MSNBC, Oct. 5, 2017

Hip hop superstar Kanye West told a shocked audience…that he didn't cast a vote in the presidential election earlier this month, but if he did, he "would have voted for Trump."
—Euan McKirdy and M. Daniel Allman, CNN, Nov. 28, 2016

In a visit to the White House ... Mr. West wore a "Make America Great Again" hat — an accessory he said that made him feel like Superman.—Katie Rogers, *New York Times*, Oct. 11, 2018

"I'm gonna say one thing. Fuck Trump!"
 —Robert DeNiro, Tony Awards, June 10, 2018

"You do know you just attacked a Gold-Star family?" one adviser warned Trump. "What's that?" he asked.
—Gabriel Sherman, *New York* Intelligencer, Oct. 29, 2016

"I think I've made a lot of sacrifices. I work very, very hard."—Donald Trump, rejecting the assertion made at the Democratic convention by Muslim lawyer Khizr Khan, whose son died in Iraq in 2004, that Trump had "sacrificed nothing and no one."
—ABC News interview, July 30, 2016

The Donald remains unraptured
By soldiers who did get captured.
He gave John McCain a zero:
Insisting, "Not a war-hero."
Showing a psyche that's fractured.

The Donald attack list is long:
Chief Justice, "Hamilton" begone;
And the Puerto Rico mayor
And also the football players—
All receive the brutal Trump bong.

Macy's, Nordstrom, the FBI,
All tagged by The Donald black fly.
Mainstream media, Meryl Streep
Join the roaring negative sweep
Of things The Donald vilifies.

Fake News, World Warming, Amazon;
Ruth Bader Ginsburg he stepped on.
Vaccines, Sanctuary Cities
Get abused in Donald's Twitties.
He shouts long list of evil spawn.

Hillary got P.J. O'Rourke's concur:
"Wrong within normal parameters."
Trump gallivants in full war paint
Parameters without restraint:
He's "Man of the People" poseur.

Trumptomium

Five Trumps interred there in Queens,
But Trump's eye is on first-hole greens.
Dropped idea of mausoleum,
Now what? Perchance coliseum.
New Jersey must approve the scene.

Trump's goal is a cemetery:
In his golf course to be buried.
Sure enough, it is a fine spot,
Not to worry about duff shots:
Bloody Marys with obituaries.

John McCain's not a war hero. He's a war hero because he was captured. I like people who weren't captured.
—Donald Trump, Family Leadership Summit, Ames, Iowa, July 18, 2015

The failure of normal empathy is central to sociopathy. Donald Trump's speech and behavior show that he has severe sociopathic traits…While there have surely been American presidents who could be said to be narcissistic; none have shown sociopathic qualities to the degree seen in Mr. Trump.
—Lance Dodes, M.D., in *The Dangerous Case of Donald Trump: 27 Psychiatrists and Mental Health Experts Assess a President* (2017)

The issue we are raising is not whether Trump is mentally ill. It is whether he is dangerous…If we are silent about the numerous ways in which Donald Trump has repeatedly threatened violence, incited violence, or boasted about his own violence, we are passively supporting and enabling the dangerous and naïve mistake of treating him as if he were a "normal" president or a "normal" political leader. He is not, and it is our duty to say so, and to say it publicly. He is unprecedentedly and abnormally dangerous.
—James Gilligan, M.D., Clinical Professor of Psychiatry and Adjunct Professor of Law, New York University, in *The Dangerous Case of Donald Trump: 27 Psychiatrists and Mental Health Experts Assess a President* (2017)

Trump has proposed different plans to be buried there over the past decade… The Donald's proposals for a mausoleum and chapel were turned down…Trump could still put his mausoleum right alongside his favorite fairway, if he can get approval from New Jersey's State Cemetery Board.
—Nancy Solomon, *New Jersey News*, Feb. 2, 2012

The flamboyant billionaire has received approval to build a private cemetery at the Trump National Golf Club, a swanky 36-hole course located in Bedminster, NJ, the Fox Business Network has learned. A spokesman for Trump…confirmed the plans for the private cemetery…
—Charlie Gasparino, Trump Digging His Own Grave, Fox Business News, July 22, 2015

But we can hope he's well aware—
Of rule even for billionaires:
No way! You can't take it with you.
He can be buried in golf shoes,
But there are no caddies to spare.

Site zoned residential dwelling;
Trump got change for his grave selling.
Given approval for land use:
Graves for club members *entre nous*.
Dead are the living expelling.

Graves open to those who have paid
Stiff fee to tee off on the glade.
This keeps Trump forever en suite
With the monetary elite—
Far from those needing Medicaid.

Burial behind the first hole;
It's the last chance for Trump control.
In the end resting in the shrubs,
Aonian rank in Trump club,
Safe from presence of any prole.

Thirty-six holes in club upscale;
The Donald figures he can't fail.
Princely fee brings eternal shrine
For people who want to recline
Forever close to his coattails.

Trumpheresis

Boundless need to be the top dog,
Trump offers endless monologue
About his really great greatness.
While we long for some sedateness.
He rants on like a demagogue.

At swearing in, Trump spoke with God,
Who gave him affirmative nod:
"We're not going to let it rain
On your speech." And wetness abstained
Or so President Trump did jaw.

Trump has been making plans to spend eternity behind the first hole of one of the courses at the Trump National Golf Club in Bedminister, New Jersey…whose members reportedly pay an initiation fee of three hundred and fifty thousand dollars.
—Jason Kersten, *The New Yorker*, Oct. 24, 2016

Trump's National Golf Course in Bedminster was transformed into a fake cemetery by activist artists to mark the President's one-year anniversary of his inauguration on Jan. 20. The activist called INDECLINE snuck onto Donald Trump's property the night of Jan. 19 to set up the elaborate and satirical "Trump Cemetery"…six headstones complete with fresh dirt to mark out the graves were placed.
—Alexis Terrazi, Patch.com, Jan 25, 2018

God looked down and he said, 'we're not going to let it rain on your speech.' In fact, when I first started, I said, oh no. The first line, I got hit by a couple of drops. And I said, oh, this is too bad…But the truth is that it stopped immediately. It was amazing. And then it became really sunny. And then I walked off and it poured right after I left. It poured.—Donald Trump Speech, CIA headquarters, Jan. 21, 2017

Mr. President, in the Bible rain is a sign of God's blessing, and it started to rain, Mr. President, when you came to the [inaugural] platform. And it's my prayer that God will bless you, your family, your administration, and may he bless America.—Evangelist Franklin Graham, Inauguration prayer, Jan. 20, 2017

Trump's wish list [for Inauguration] included Elton John, Aretha Franklin, and Paul Anka—who, he hoped, would sing "My Way"—but they all claimed to be otherwise engaged.
—Patrick Radden Keefe, *The New Yorker*, Jan. 7, 2019

Private physician reflected,
Healthiest ever elected.
Others do question the mental
As definitely fragmental.
Overdue to be inspected.

Passing mental test, Trump did crow:
He could name camel and hippo.
A test for signs of dementia,
No proof of vanguard potentia.
What does his hippocampus show?

Oval Office: open to all—
Yes, even to total screwballs.
No psych test required to be passed;
Narcissus quotient's never asked.
Vainglory brings no curtain call.

Living in realm Trumplandia,
Ruler vibe of hydrangea.
So hostile to science and art,
Those hoping for life a la carte
Must leave for Fennoscondia.

Trump bragged he could take out a gun
On Fifth Avenue, shoot someone,
And legions would still vote for him.
No one says his ego is slim;
Claims this remark hit a home run.

Tony Soprano told his shrink
Of his truly terrible kink:
"Fucking King Midas in reverse."
Trump behavior also perverse:
All things he touches start to stink.

Countless mental-health pros declare
Psycho in Oval Office chair.
Future conditions named for him:
Trumptia, Trumposis, Trumpshim.
 Let's get him the needed health care.

[He will be] the healthiest individual ever elected to the presidency.—Harold Bornstein, Trump personal physician for 25 years, Dec. 14, 2015

He's got perfect genes. He has incredible energy and he's unbelievably healthy.—Stephen Mnunchin, Secretary of Treasury to Mike Allen, *Axios*, March 26, 2017

Trump is amoral…Amoral is when you shoot someone in the head, it doesn't make a difference. No conscience.
—Retired Senator Henry Reid, in Mark Leibovich, *New York Times*, Jan. 2, 2019

For the first time, America has a president who does not act like an adult. He is emotionally immature: he taunts, insults, bullies, rages, seeks vengeance, exalts violence, boasts, refuses to accept criticism. —James Mann, *The New York Review of Books*, Oct. 26, 2017

It's a shame the White House has become an adult day care center. Someone obviously missed their shift this morning.
—Senator Bob Corker, Republican chairman of the Foreign Relations Committee and early supporter of Donald Trump's candidacy, Twitter, Oct. 8, 2017

'I could stand in the middle of Fifth Avenue and shoot people and I wouldn't lose voters.' Trump said in a rally in Iowa, pointing his finger at the crowd like he was shooting a handgun.
—Newsday.com staff, Sioux Center, Iowa, Jan. 23, 2016

Everyone with half a brain and a recent copy of the DSM (the *Diagnostic and Statistical Manual of Mental Disorders*, used by shrinks everywhere) knew the diagnosis on Trump the instant he joined the race. Trump fits the clinical definition of a narcissistic personality so completely that it will be a shock if future psychiatrists don't rename the disorder after him. —Matt Taibbi, *Rolling Stone*, Sept. 19, 2017

My twitter has become so powerful that I can actually make my enemies tell the truth.
—@realDonaldTrump, Twitter, Oct. 27, 2012

I can't help it that I'm a celebrity. What am I going to do, hide under a stone?—Donald Trump to Mark Singer, *The New Yorker*, May 19, 1997

TV show rescued this D-lister;
Public loved this ethics-twister
Serially bankrupt galoot
Finds his zone with rooty-toot-toot.
Now we need to find resisters.

To achieve his "Apprentice" fame
Trump showed all how to play the game.
"You're fired": his best keynoted phrase;
Becoming a popular craze.
We need it now—to end mass shame.

The Economist described him
With statements altogether grim:
"Utterly unfit for office."
It's of no use to pray for us:
We need an Impeachment prelim.

Some say he is a Hitler clone,
Or a discard from Twilight Zone.
Let's just stop the Fiddle-de-dee;
We don't have time to wait and see.
Line up now and demand "Dethrone!"

Yes, a crisis has arisen:
Oval Office needs revision.
We don't require a bulldozer
To stop the moral rollover.
Read: Constitution provision.

Nothing there that he can gainsay:
What we need is Impeachment Day.
Time to show him the White House gate;
He can slink back to real estate.
Fire him! Don't don't don't don't delay.

With "The Apprentice," the TV producer mythologized Trump—then a floundering d-lister—as the ultimate titan... [T]he entire premise of "The Apprentice" was ... something of a con. ... 'The Apprentice' portrayed Trump [a serially bankrupt carnival barker] as a plutocrat with impeccable business instincts... —Patrick Radden Keefe, *The New Yorker*, Jan. 7, 2019

"I'm being truthful, and I'll always be truthful," one ["Apprentice"] contestant protests in fifth season premiere, and Trump's response, as he turns to dismiss her, is telling. "How stupid is that?"—Mark Brennan, Paste, June 29, 2016

"Let me tell you, the one that matters is me."
—Donald Trump, interview, Fox News, Nov. 2, 2017

I went from VERY successful businessman, to top T.V. Star...to President of the United States (on my first try). I think that would qualify as not smart, but genius...and a very stable genius at that!
—@realDonaldTrump, Twitter, Jan. 6, 2018

[W]e're talking about a president who is seriously interested in the idea of doing all the jobs in the White House himself.
—Ben Mathis-Lilley, The Slatest, March 29, 2018

Calls to the White House switchboard during this Christmas holiday are greeted by a recorded message stating they can't take calls: "The government has shut down."
—December 24, 2018

There are no committees by election, but only committees for work. All committees are subjected to the leader and not he to the committees. He decides.
—Adolf Hitler, *Mein Kamp* (1929, 20th edition 1999)

Trump-Speak

I am the ruler of the land,
The monarch of the high command
 Whose praise the world loudly high-fives.
And we are his daughters, & his sons & his wives!
And we are his daughters & his sons & his wives!

At Twitter, see how high I ride,
My bosom, it does swell with pride,
And I snap my fingers at a critic's derides.
And so do my daughters & my sons & my wives!
And so do my daughters & my sons & my wives !

What's the big deal about the Russians?
Sure I have lots of discussions,
I say it's time for the media's deep-six dive.
And so say my daughters & my sons & my wives!
And so say my daughters & my sons & my wives!

For policy domestic and foreign
I don't need an advisor warren.
From my own mind wisdom arrives.
And so say my daughters & my sons & my wives!
And so say my daughters & my sons & my wives!

And when the abuse rolls in
I have a staff to do the spin—
And the seclusion a golf course provides.
And so do my daughters & my sons & my wives!
And so do my daughters & my sons & my wives!

I just stick with Fox News truth—
Straight from them to the voting booth.
I don't care about left-wing knives,
Neither do my daughters or my sons or my wives!
Neither do my daughters or my sons or my wives!

If Mueller's snooping hardens.
I'll be ready with the pardons:
Always there with my bare Id
For me, myself, I, and Jared,
And for my daughters and my sons and my wives!

II TRUMPLOOT:
In Midas He Trusts

Trumpocracy complication:
Excess of family station.
Ignoring all moral clutter,
No concern where bread gets buttered.
Now! Ethics resuscitation.

Fans value Trumpster's able guile;
He gives them much reason to smile.
Some may insist he's a dodo;
Lots cheer wheeler-dealer mojo
And his frantic ego turnstile.

"Trump *über* alles!" gobs admire,
Gleeful as Mainstream goes haywire.
Trump's done more than offer a poke
To logjam politico yokes,
While press roasts on funeral pyres.

With OJ in gold-trimmed glasses,
Trump does brag he's modern Midas;
No mention of big debt boo-boos.
Those who prove reverse, he does sue,
Clutching rod of regal fasces.

Trump sees Tower as the grand prix:
We see over-the-top gaudy.
Much of Louis XIV tableau
Vies in luxe with Versailles Chateau.
Faux coats of arms: id apogee.

Claimed a worth of $9.5 billion.
Research tagged it under $300 million.
Trump said sources were jealous guys
Beset with four-hundred-pound wives.
Outed, he becomes reptilian.

Money-makers are tiresome company, as they have no standard but cash value." — Plato, *The Republic*

It's very possible that I could be the first presidential candidate to run and make money on it.
—Donald J. Trump, *Fortune*, April 3, 2000

It has not been easy for me. It has not been easy for me. I started off in Brooklyn. My father gave me a small loan of a million dollars.—Donald Trump, Town Hall Event, Atkinson, NH, Oct. 26, 2015

Fred Trump lent his son at least $60.7 million, or $140 million in today's dollars. Much of it was never repaid, records show.
— Russ Buettner, Susanne Craig, & David Barstow, *New York Times*, Oct. 2, 2018

A judge in New Jersey dismissed a $5 billion defamation lawsuit filed by Donald J. Trump against an author [Timothy L. O'Brien] whose book placed Mr. Trump's personal wealth far below his public estimates.
—Peter S. Goodman, *New York Times*, July 15, 2009

Mr. Trump's American coat of arms belongs to another family. It was granted by British authorities in 1939 to Joseph Edward Davies, the third husband of Marjorie Merriweather Post, the socialite who build the Mar-a-Lago resort… The Trump organization took Mr. Davies's coat of arms for its own, making one small adjustment—replacing the word "Integritas"…with "Trump."
—Danny Hakins, *New York Times,* May 28, 2017

[A] critic called his Trump Tower penthouse "Louis XIV on LSD" and Donald himself compared his painted chapel there to Michelangelo's Sistine Chapel.—Conrad Black, *Donald J. Trump: A President Like No Other* (2018)

"Too underwater" nixed foreclosure.
Later in so-called disclosure,
Claimed he knows how to handle debt.
Owing billions causes no sweat,
He tries to strong-arm exposure.

Trump Taj Mahal, with minarets,
Striped domes and flashing lights beset,
In Chapter 11 wreckage.
Funders lost big: Trump kept checkage.
For him, bankruptcy brings no fret.

Taj was erected on large land
Cleared with government nod and hand
For some affordable housing,
Not for casino carousing.
Trump never complied with this plan.

Multiple bankruptcies: Count 'em;
But nosedives do not make Trump glum;
He's the smart guy who stands aloft,
Trumpeting of his umpteen boffs,
Leaving others to sweep the crumbs.

When The Donald owed some billions,
Claimed banks danced to his cotillion.
Seventy-two banks revised loans
Tell the tale of that Davy Jones:
Of ethic lacertilian.

What of the Trump brand in Turkey?
The deal is darker than murky,
With advisor Flynn on the ropes.
Let's ask about those envelopes
Of dough that some do call perky.

That hotel in Azerbaijan:
Chummy project for a con man.
Mannadov bought use of Trump name.
Hotel's closed, skirting shame,
But Ivanka's on Instagram.

Trump's gargantuan vampire empire had helped give the town [Atlantic City] its Third World economic flavor—its cash product siphoned out for use elsewhere, its casino enclave arrayed against a skyline of wilting poverty like desert mirages.—Wayne Barrett, *Trump: The Greatest Show on Earth* (1992)

[H]igh rollers could sleep off their losses in the Alexander the Great Suite for $10,000 a night.—Timothy O'Brien, *TrumpNation: The Art of Being The Donald* (2005)

The second floor of the Taj Mahal was labeled as the 14th on the elevator panel. The elevator climbed from there to the top, the "51st" floor, in reality the 42nd floor.
—Chris Hedges, *America: The Farewell Tour* (2018)

Trump denied the bankruptcy was a setback: "I don't think it's a failure, it's a success," he said. "In this case, it was just something that worked better than other alternatives. It's really just a technical thing, but it came together."
—Associated Press, Nov. 22, 2004

"Fourth Time's A Charm: How Donald Trump Made Bankruptcy Work For Him"
—Clare O'Connor, *Forbes*, April 29, 2011

Trump hired over one thousand lawyers to hammer out an agreement to keep the banks from collecting on the $3.2 billion he owed.
—Chris Hedges, *America: The Farewell Tour* (2018)

I have never gone bankrupt by the way. I have never.
—Donald J. Trump, Republican debate, Aug. 6, 2015

A shareholder who bought $100 of DFT shares in 1995 could sell them for about $4 in 2005…as its chief executive Trump was paid more than $44 million.
—Michael Kranish & Marc Fisher, *Trump Revealed: An American Journey of Ambition, Ego, Money, and Power* (2016)

It's always good to do things nice and complicated so that nobody can figure it out.—Donald J. Trump to Mark Singer, *The New Yorker*, May 19, 1997

Now this is very Yugely clear:
Trump insulates himself from fear.
Whether holdings prosper or not,
He finds way to hook money pot.
Hail and laud slimeball marketeer!

Golf course worth based on who's asking;
Trump disputes property taxing.
Public records show his dissent
Lowers price by 97 percent,
Locals suffer his gain maxing.

Bought huge yacht from Sultan Brunei
Who wore a different old school tie.
Added disco, hundreds of phones,
What was missing was golden throne,
Still, it was a bobbing Versailles.

Boat no topic of flotation;
Whose is larger? Trump fixation.
With not a care for Beaufort Scale.
He did not buy the boat to sail—
Just for macho demonstration.

Loot got short: Trump headed for fall;
Boat sold to Al-Waleed bin Talal,
A Saudi prince with lots of dough.
Sale greatly helped Trump's money flow
And freed him for more moolah sprawl.

This billionaire Prince bin Talal
Was later by Trump so appalled,
Calling candidate a disgrace
For his campaign Muslim debase.
Engaged in fiery Twitter brawl.

Now in power shift with Saudis
With whom Trump has long said "Howdy."
Eleven princes arrested.
Trump still continues invested
With money trail kinda cloudy.

Trump's fortunes derive from his mastery of the con. As he skipped around his creditors during the bankruptcy of his casinos, the courts put him on a personal budget: $450,000 a month, affirming the success of his fuck-you/gimme-gimme attitude toward the system.
—Michael Sorkin, *The Nation*, July 26, 2016

[M]y serious problems with Malcolm [Forbes] didn't start until I bought a magnificent yacht. Malcolm's 150-foot yacht was legendary—until I came along with a much more luxurious 282-foot yacht, and stole the spotlight away.
—Donald J. Trump, *Trump: Surviving at the Top* (1990)

When that *Forbes* cover story on me ran, I looked at the unfair estimates of my assets…and shook my head. This wasn't journalism…this was Malcolm finally getting back at me from the grave, with the help of his family, especially his son Steve.
—Donald J. Trump, *Trump: Surviving at the Top* (1990)

The Saudi prince was younger and much richer than Trump… He poured money into Citicorp, Disney, and the Plaza Hotel.
—Michael D'Antonio, *Never Enough: Donald Trump and the Pursuit of Success* (2015)

@realDonaldTrump You are a disgrace not only to the GOP but to all America
— @Alwaleed_Talal, Twitter, Dec. 11, 2015

President elect @realDonaldTrump whatever the past differences, America has spoken, congratulations & best wishes.—@Alwaleed_Talal, Twitter, Nov. 9, 2016

Lobbyists representing the Saudi government reserved blocks of rooms at President Trump's Washington, D.C., hotel within a month of Trump's election in 2016 — paying for an estimated 500 nights at the luxury hotel in just three months.—David A. Fahrenthold & Jonathan O'Connell, *Washington Post*, Dec. 6, 2018

The Trump International Hotel recently took in about $270,000 in payments tied to the Kingdom of Saudi Arabia…Last month, Trump visited Saudi Arabia, the first stop on the first foreign trip of the presidency.
—Fredricka Schouten, *USA Today*, June 5, 2017

Trump Shuttle: "Diamond in the sky,"
Golden fixtures did typify.
Didn't take long for it to tank.
With debt split among twenty banks:
Diamond revealed as louse fly.

Trumpoline

SoHo launch most lavish ever.
Doormen's powdered wigs deemed clever.
Alex Sapir dubbed it sexy
But it's ended up chachexy,
A very shady endeavor.

Trump SoHo offered weird abode.
Calling it hotel skirted code.
Place zoned for manufacturing,
The dwelling rules were fracturing,
And Russian occupancy slowed.

Unit went for million or more,
But you needed to know the score.
Can't be lived in by same party
For much of year. Not so smarty
For those not in one-percent corps.

Strumming on Kazakhstan banjo,
Trump worked this deal on TV show.
Partners included shady mob,
Joining him in the money lob,
Trying hard to launder the dough,

The Institute of Architects
Refused to bow or genuflect
But named it a banal glass box.
Not fitting in with nearby blocks.
A wretched region disconnect.

When excavators found some bones
Deep inside an old church vault zone,
Trump project only briefly jarred.
Yes, skyscraper built on graveyard.
Never fear: Commerce does move stones.

Trump's airline dalliance appears to have been airbrushed from his official biography… As former Trump Shuttle president Bruce Nobles told *The Daily Beast*, "I cringed every time he opened his mouth."
—Barbara Peterson, The Daily Beast, Oct. 4, 2015

The [SoHo] building…was explicitly marketed to perspective buyers overseas as a second or third home, with the challenging proviso that owners could live in their apartments only 120 days a year, and never for more than 29 consecutive days in any 36-day period.
—Craig Unger, *Vanity Fair,* Aug. 13, 2017

The building, which includes…"Ivanka's Choice" facial for $370…bath products encrusted in faux diamonds…a $25 packet of milk chocolate nuggets shaped like gold bullion with TRUMP stamped in the candy…has lost revenue… and slashed prices… shedding more guests with each controversy involving the White House.
—Sarah Maslin Nir, *New York Times*, Nov. 23, 2017

Since the 1990s, some $1.3 trillion in illicit capital had poured out of Russia, meaning that hordes of cash needed to be laundered…Trump SoHo has been involved in on-going litigation, including a lawsuit claiming that it was partly financed from "questionable sources"…from Russia and Kazakhstan.
—Craig Unger, *Vanity Fair,* Aug. 13, 2017

Partners on the project included Soviet-born businessman Felix Sater and Tevfik Arif, who ran the Bayrock Group real estate development firm. Sater had a history of running afoul of the law.—collaboration between *ProPublica*, WNYC, and *The New Yorker*, Oct. 4, 2017

Trump and Bayrock partnered with the Sapir Organization…in the development of Trump SoHo. Alex Sapir's business partner Rotem Rosen is a former lieutenant of the Soviet-born Israeli billionaire Lev Leviev, an oligarch with longstanding ties to Vladimir Putin who counts the Russian president as a "true friend."
—Ben Schreckinger, *Politico*, Aug. 26, 2016

"Our boy can become president of the USA and we can engineer it," Felix Sater wrote in November 2015. "I will get all of Putin's team to buy in on this, I will manage this process."—note to Michael Cohen in Morgan Chalfant, *The Hill*, Jan. 6, 2019

Here a condo, there a condo,
Russian buyers just some John Does.
Some guys from Russia, who does know?
That's just the way real estate goes:
Meenie Miney VladimirDough.

SoHo in post-election slink
As non-Ruskies feared Trump stink.
Trump paid to remove his dipstick.
SoHo now called The Dominick,
Owners hope for image uplink.

Trump withholds any disclosures
On all his many foreclosures.
This big time real estate tycoon
Is in fact a spermatozoon,
Hiding out in golf enclosures.

Here's a favored Trumped-up ditty:
"Made dough in Atlantic City."
It was real big-time bankruptcy,
Leaving before the necropsy;
Ever others stuck with kitty.

Millions past due to contractors;
Lots more to bank benefactors.
Low-balled Sinatra on Taj hire;
Frank told Trump to self-F**k aspire.
Trump at ease with sludge extractor.

It was a deal in chumps not chips,
And new owner make a great flip.
Hard Rock did scrap Taj minarets
And lent each guest guitar with frets.
After The Donald's debt was stripped.

Heads rolled in real estate sections:
Citibank and Chase saw flexions.
Heaps of veeps fired: idiocy—
Handing out dough hideously.
The Donald saw no abjection.

A Reuters review has found that at least 63 individuals with Russian passports or addresses have bought at least $98.4 million worth of property in seven Trump-branded luxury towers in southern Florida.
—Reuters Special Report, March 17, 2017

Pelosi Says She Will Skip Trump and Negotiate Directly With Putin. "I'm avoiding the middleman," she said.
—Andy Borowitz, *The New Yorker*, January 5, 2019

The emerging world in general attributes such brand premium to real estate that we are going all over the place, primarily Russia.—Donald Trump, Jr, executive vice-president of Development and Acquisitions for the Trump Organization.
—e-TurboNews, Sept. 15, 2008

At least 60 lawsuits, along with hundreds of liens, judgments, and other government filings reviewed by the USA TODAY NETWORK, document people who have accused Trump and his businesses of failing to pay them for their work. Among them: A dishwasher in Florida. An executive vice president of Development and Acquisitions for the Trump Organization. A glass company in New Jersey. A carpet company. A plumber. Painters. Forty-eight waiters. Dozens of bartenders and other hourly workers at his resorts and clubs, coast to coast. Real estate brokers who sold his properties. And, ironically, several law firms that once represented him in these suits and others.—Steve Reilly, *USA Today*, June 9, 2016

Donald J. Trump's Taj Mahal casino in Atlantic City has filed for Chapter 11 bankruptcy protection in a prearranged deal with creditors to reduce its $675 million "junk bond" debt. The $1 billion Taj Mahal opened last year.
—Reuters, July 18, 1993

The Trump Taj Mahal casino broke anti-money laundering rules 106 times in its first year and a half of operation in the early 1990s, according to the IRS in a 1998 settlement agreement.
—Jose Pagliery, CNN, May 22, 2017

The Trump Taj Mahal, the casino that the real estate mogul built for $1.2 billion in 1990, went for 4 cents on the dollar when it was sold in March.
—Associated Press, May 9, 2017

As always, he lies about size:
High-rise floors tricky enterprise.
Forty-one becomes fifty-one,
And Donald calls it a home run.
One more way to capitalize.

At time when *Playboy* was still awed:
"Daunting entrepreneur" applaud—
With Vanderbilts, Whitneys, Astors.
Trump yakked just faster and faster
About self as deal-making god.

Trumpoma

Deal: stretch limos luxurious,
Trump Series Gold trim serious,
Trim, handles, external badging.
The Donald ended up cadging:
Vowed buy of fifty spurious.

Nobody else wanted car deal:
An opulent office-on-wheels.
With inlaid Trump crest on the seats,
Surely quite unique on the street,
With paper-shredder nonpareil.

And there's Trump University,
With standards not even cursory.
Shouting promises grandiose,
Leaving students fully morose,
Mind and money adversity.

Trump sales team ranked student assets:
Then came the loud blare of trumpets.
Students who bought the $1,495 course
Were pumped to $34,995 endorse.
Micro course content, macro debt.

In a try for even more loot,
Changed the name to Wealth Institute.
Then courts declared pure trumpery,
Judged complete huckster flummery.
Trump enterprises got the boot.

Playboy: Then what does all this—the yacht, the bronze tower, the casino—really mean to you?
Trump: Props for the show.
Playboy: And what is the show?
Trump: The show is "Trump" and it is sold-out performances everywhere. I've had fun doing it and will continue to have fun, and I think most people enjoy it.
—Glenn Plaskin, *Playboy*, March 1990

Trump got in touch with Cadillac…to design nothing short of 'the most opulent stretch limousine made'…The entrepreneurs like Trump with approximately the same taste in cars as Trump, an admittedly small circle of people.
—Autoweek.com, Jan. 13, 2017

At the time, Trump remarked of the cars: "You can see the kind of quality there is. We left nothing out. I'm very honored that they built me the first one and, frankly, I deserve it."
—Davey D. Johnson, *Car and Driver*, Jan. 4, 2017

Politicians often charge their opponents with selling snake oil when they overpromise. But in litigation that has been meandering through court for years, Trump is being accused of actually selling snake oil. That term was used intermittently with Cobra Sexual Energy supplements during the hearing as shorthand for describing a worthless product that would more easily lend itself to a class-action case, because all the buyers would be entitled to a full refund.—Steven Brill, "What the Legal Battle Over Trump University Reveals About Its Founder," *Time*, Nov 5, 2015

A coat-of-arms, even a university motto: "Greed est bonum."—*Doonesbury* cartoon

A judge has finalized a $25 million dollar settlement in the Trump University class action lawsuit…In November 2016, just days after the election, Trump agreed to settle three lawsuits filed against his real estate school that argued the program featured false advertisements and empty promises.
—Doug Criss, CNN, April 10, 2018

New York State filed $40 million suit
For the Trump course con attribute
And for the massive student scam:
Promised T-bone but served up spam.
Post-election Trump parachute.

Trumpride

Boasting loudly of his great coin,
Trump crows abut tax code purloin.
Not paying taxes "makes me smart."
Yes, a fine message to impart—
A fine king cobra to conjoin.

Trump Inter. Hotel and Tower,
Quite a nice Vancouver bower.
Financed by Vnescheconombank.
Question it and Trump will pull rank
Just sitting silent with glower.

At ribbon-cutting, Junior there,
With Ivanka, Eric, and, yes, *pére*.
In mortgage default, buyers sued.
Dupes of investment scheme they rued.
Just a name sell; ignore repair.

Asked of isolationism,
Which could cause a Euro schism,
"We're a powerful company,"
Trump replied—"eh—eh—eh—country."
Some more psychic botulism.

Russian money here, money there,
Russian money is everywhere.
Take a look at Trump's campaign stream
And at his cabinet A-team.
Russian money is everywhere.

Winter White House of 110,000 sq feet:
Sweetheart dealers The Donald greets.
Yuge enough for the Trump ego,
While spreading mental serpigo.
Three bomb shelters make it complete.

According to the New York State attorney general, Trump University was a "straight up fraud…a fraud from beginning to end."—Nick Gass, *Politico*, Sept. 25, 2016

The Wall Street Journal estimated that Trump's guarantees could exceed $600 million. In one astonishing decade, Donald Trump had become the Brazil of Manhattan.
—*Vanity Fair,* September 1990

What we do know is that Trump has in fact manipulated financial records to cheat on his obligation to the government.—David Cay Johnston, *It's Even Worse Than You Think: What The Trump Administration Is Doing to America* (2018)

"The stars have all aligned," Eric Trump, who as executive vice president of the Trump Organization oversees all its golf properties, said on Thursday morning, while sipping an iced tea at the restaurant inside the Trump International Hotel… "I think our brand is the hottest it has ever been." — Eric Lipton & Susanne Craig, *New York Times*, March 9, 2017

A Reuters investigation found that at least 63 individuals with Russian passports or addresses bought $98.4 million worth of property in seven Trump-branded towers in Florida.—Luke Harding, *Collusion: Secret Meetings, Dirty Money, and How Russia Helped Donald Trump Win* (2017)

If [Donald] smoked, he'd have his cigarettes monogrammed like so—$—with Ayn Rand's dollar sign.—Liz Smith, *Natural Blonde* (2000)

Meet and greet at Mar-a-Lago,
No care how Constitution go.
Emolument Clauses ignore,
Bury the law under the floor.
Schmooze and swag at Sap-a-Sago.

But there is also a down side
To all this deep bountiful tide.
Some charity events cancelled
From the Trump name to unspancel.
Aid came: Trump sister coax applied.

At all those other golf courses
Trump family has its own bourses.
Lobbyists pay for membership
And watch benefits drip, drip, drip.
From consiglieri forces.

Trump money card was even played
In inaugural motorcade.
Stopping in front of Trump Hotel,
Family emerged for a sell,
Showing world their balance of trade.

Want to incentivize Trump grace?
Rent pricey rooms at DC place.
Ambassadors and foundations
Find this to be a swell station
For showing off their Trump embrace.

And Trump's media grandstanding
Brought international branding:
Russia, Argentina, Dubai—
Many deep pocketed allies.
Emoluments bring cash landing.

Towers in Turkey and Mumbai
Heighten questions about allies.
A blind trust not his cup of tea;
Manages them for hefty fees.
Time for U.S. to shout, "BYE-BYE!"

Mar-a-Lago, the Palm Beach resort owned by the Trump Organization, doubled its initiation fee to $200,000 following the election of Donald Trump as president…Members also pay $14,000 a year in annual dues [and an annual food minimum of $2,000].—Robert Frank, CNBC, Jan. 25, 2017

President Trump's Mar-a-Lago Club, which lost 19 charity events to cancellations amid controversy about his political rhetoric, has booked a new gala event—put on by a small, previously dormant charity that was encouraged to use the site by Trump's sister.
—David A. Fahrenthold, *Washington Post*, Nov. 30, 2017

Trump's travel to Mar-a-Lago alone probably cost taxpayers more than $64 million.—Philip Bump, *Washington Post*, Feb. 5, 2019

In another oratorical high point, the president managed, in a speech about the evils of North Korea, to work in a plug for one of his properties. ("The Women's US Open was held this year at Trump national Golf Club in Bedminster, NJ, and it just happened to be won by a great Korean golfer…")
—Gail Collins, *New York Times*, Nov. 9, 2017

[A]t Trump's Washington hotel the average revenue per guest night was $653. That was triple the average of all district of Columbia hotels…Tabs were run up by lobbyists, executives, foreign diplomats, and other favor seekers with deep expense accounts who found it the best place to meet Trump cabinet members and other appointees with their own deep pockets.—David Cay Johnston, *It's Even Worse Than You Think: What The Trump Administration Is Doing to America* (2018)

"The fact that the inaugural committee did business with the Trump Organization raises huge ethical questions about the potential for undue enrichment," said Marcus Owens, the former head of the division of the Internal Revenue Service that oversees nonprofits.—Ilya Marritz & Justin Eliott, Truthdig, Dec. 14, 2018

At least 50 executives of companies that bagged sweetheart government contracts, as well as 21 lobbyists and trade group officials, are members of Trump golf courses in Florida, New Jersey, and Virginia.—Brad Penzenstadler & Aamer Madhani, *USA Today*, Sept. 6, 2017

Why let this rich family Trump
Abuse us flat out as fool chumps?
Congress has power to flag down
And turn out emoluments clown.
Send this pickpocket to the dump.

Set-up as a nation of rules.
Gives us huge statutory tools:
Life, liberty, and happiness—
And to get rid of crappiness.
Stop being played as YUGE fools.

Emoluments now.
Dump the Trump!
Dump the Trump!
Dump the Trump!

> The Trump Organization, the Trump Foundation, the Trump family, the Trump campaign, the Trump transition, the Trump inauguration, and the Trump White House are all being probed for wrongdoing.
> —Timothy L. O'Brien, BloombergOpinion, Dec. 17, 2018

III TRUMPOTICA:
The Women in His Life

There was a crude man of New York
Who treated all ladies like pork.
With specific money supplied,
Companions did run alongside
That rich, old crude man of New York.

Off from Gotti and Fat Tony,
Roy Cohn fixed pre-alimony.
It was Czech mate at the altar
With Cohn's pre-nuptial halter,
Advising Trump parsimony.

Reception at 21 Club,
Once speakeasy, then all-star hub.
Roy Cohn was there and Mayor Beame,
And lots of folk who moved upstream.
Joey Adams emceed the nub.

After three kids and bankruptcies.
The Donald wanted tangencies.
The Marble Collegiate Church
Did became an amorous perch
For some new horny valencies.

Wedlock could have only one ace,
And so Ivana got replaced.
She declares for the world to know
In raising kids, she ran the show,
And flourished in the marketplace.

The pair gave varied press versions
For bang-up public diversion.
No thought of what children could make
Of roaring marital earthquake
With its thundery aspersions.

Trump: You really want to know what I consider ideal company?
Me: Yes
Trump: A total piece of ass.
—Mark Singer, *The New Yorker*, April 25, 2011

What surprises many people is that beautiful women love me…I have been able to date (screw) them all because I have something that many men do not have.—Donald J. Trump & Bill Zanker, *Think Big: Make It Happen in Business and Life* (2007)

Roy Cohn urged Donald to begin married life with codified financial arrangements…Cohn's proposal called on Ivana to return any gifts from Donald in the event of a divorce. In response to her fury, Cohn added language allowing her to keep her clothing, and any gifts.—Michael Kranish & Mark Fisher, *Trump Revealed: An American Journey of Ambition, Ego, Money, and Power* (2016)

Often in Marble Collegiate Church on Fifth Avenue, where Donald and Ivana were married [and where his father's funeral service was held]…he and Marla rendezvoused. "Not that we went together, but we would both be there on occasion.—Marla Maples in Maureen Orth, *Vanity Fair*, November 1990

I was too successful to be Mrs. Trump. In our marriage, there couldn't be two stars. So one of us had to go.
—Ivana Trump, *Raising Trump (2017)*

Why had I hung in there so long when things were just not what they should have been. My marriage, it seemed, was the only arc of my life in which I was willing to accept something less than perfection.
—Donald J. Trump, *Trump: Surviving at the Top (1990)*

Trumpitch

Ere donning his "values" dog tags,
"You can do anything," he brags.
"Grab 'em by pussy," advice is.
Move on her "like a bitch:" prizes.
Sordid swagger of two-bit stag.

He wrote in *TRUMP: How to Get Rich*
How dames on "The Apprentice" twitch.
"All the women flirted with me...
That's to be expected." Whoopee!
Bottom feeder machismo pitch.

He wrote to bring home the dinner
Sex appeal was the clear winner.
His often-used contestant test
Was the size of a woman's breasts:
Trump the ever-shagging spinner.

With fidgety sex chromosome,
He did bring this creepiness home,
With some grotesque psychodrama,
Putting pretty young Ivanka
In ghastly observation dome.

He liked to brag to Howard Stern
All about young Ivanka's burn.
He said things he should not oughter:
"If Ivanka weren't my daughter..."
And all decorum he did spurn.

Howard Stern asked, "Can I say this?
Ivanka is a piece of ass."
Trump agreed, taking no affront
And even offering a punt
On post-30, women's prime pass.

Also bragged on radio loud
That Ivanka was well-endowed
Said there's no need for a bust boost
For curvaceous pride of his roost.
She's got it, so shirk any shroud.

All the women on "The Apprentice" flirted with me—consciously or unconsciously. That's to be expected. It's certainly not groundbreaking news that early victories by the women on "The Apprentice" were, to a very large extent, dependent on their sex appeal.
—Donald J. Trump & Meredith McIver, *Trump: How to Get Rich* (2004)

In the middle of conversations he would pull out [Marla's picture and rhapsodize about her physical endowments. Sometimes he would interrupt meetings in his conference room and put up a videotape of her for everyone to watch. There she'd be in a bathing suit jiggling around and he'd be making all these comments about 'nice tits, no brains.'
— Gwenda Blair, *Donald Trump: The Candidate* (2000)

Mr. Trump frequently sought assurances—at times from strangers—that the women in his life were beautiful. During the 1997 Miss Teen USA pageant, he sat in the audience as his teenage daughter, Ivanka, helped to host the event from onstage. He turned to Brook Antoinette Mahealani Lee, Miss Universe at the time, and asked for her opinion of his daughter's body. 'Don't you think my daughter's hot? She's hot, right?" Ms Lee recalled him saying.
"I was like, 'Really?' That's just weird. She was 16. That's creepy."
—Michael Barbaro & Megan Twohey, *New York Times*, May 14, 2016

You know who's one of the great beauties of the world, according to everybody? And I helped create her—Ivanka.
—Donald Trump on Howard Stern Show, 20003

She does have a very nice figure. I've said if Ivanka weren't my daughter, perhaps I'd be dating her.
—Donald Trump, "The View," March 6, 2006

In her book, Ivanka advised
That women do need to apprise
Between harassment and just tease,
Which is so easy to appease.
Says, Don't be too quick to chastise.

As owner of Miss Universe,
With nude women Trump did converse.
Of beauty shows, his was spicy.
And his conduct, it was dicey,
Bad behavior he did disperse.

He bought pageant Miss USA,
And had one message to convey:
"Higher heels; smaller bathing suits!"
Give that man a Rooty-Toot-Toot!
Always eager for some horseplay.

Maybe babe Marla panted it,
Or maybe Donald planted it.
The Post headline widely-quoted:
"Best Sex I've Ever Had!" noted.
And of course Donald chanted it.

Layette wear brand in November;
Plaza wedding in December.
Bankers sore about cost of ring:
But Henry Winston lent the bling.
Tiffany new household member.

Trump Taj Mahal had wedding chip:
Just one more piece of salesmanship.
Trump felt boredom in wedding aisle—
Just another Donald Turnstile—
Soon handing Marla a pink slip.

Trumpick

Young blondes in the Trump arena
Offering bravura scena.
But everything Donald touches
Gets marked by plenty of smutches.
Bits of bedraggled patina.

Ivanka Trump says that as kids, she and her brothers learned the tawdry details of their parents' scandalous divorce by reading *The Post*. "We'd come home from school having read [about] them on the cover of *The Post*," she reveals. The most jolting possibly being "Marla Boasts to Pals About Donald: BEST SEX I EVER HAD."
—Staff, *New York Post*, June 18, 2008

The real estate developer and the Georgia Peach haven't set the date yet…but she's sporting a new diamond that's as big as the Plaza. No, bigger…No one's saying how much it cost or whether The Donald had to ask his bankers before he could ask Marla.
—Janna Barron, *New York Times*, July 4, 1991

Where, [bankers] demanded to know, had he gotten the money for the $250,000 ring? Trump skated past their ire. The ring, he said, was on loan, borrowed from the jeweler Harry Winston in exchange for free publicity.—Michael Kranish and Marc Fisher, *Trump Revealed: An American Journey of Ambition, Ego, Money, and Power* (2016)

That woman knowingly entered into a relationship with my husband, the father of three small children. She actively participated in humiliating me in the media and indirectly put my kids at risk for months. I went through hell.
—Ivana Trump, *Raising Trump* (2017)

The middle-aged master builder finally decides to marry the actress-model mother of his infant child, a week after she unveils her new line of maternity clothes, in a ceremony at the grand hotel formerly managed by his former wife.
—Todd S. Purdum, *New York Times,* Dec. 18, 1993

I came from Georgia, family values and strong sense of spiritual growth…After some years we realized we had to move on…I'm a Southern girl.—Marla Maples, "Access Hollywood," April 16, 2016

Trump liked to say that one of the things that made life worth living was… more or less constant sexual banter. "Do you still like having sex with your wife? How often? You must have had a better f*** than your wife?" ... All the while, Trump would have his friend's wife on the speakerphone, listening in.
—Michael Wolff, *Fire and Fury, Inside the Trump White House* (2018)

Sees letch role as no sour pickle;
Trump's sure people are quite tickled.
Calls racy love life "fantasy,"
Certainly not a travesty.
People like him to be fickle.

Twice-divorced, hit on Brooke Shields.
Twenty years younger, still the spiel;
"Let's' date: you're the sweetheart
And I'm the richest man." Love dart
On the Trump amorous hayfield.

Trump does brag about his beachhead:
"I've never had trouble in bed."
One regret: Never did date Diana.
Give the man a big banana—
And please prescribe some needed meds.

Trump 101: The Way to Success
Offered this Trumpian access:
 "Women are like buildings."
And he does like lots of gilding
With oodles of ways for egress.

To media, touting memoir,
Ivana says she's still a star.
Now she calls herself "first lady,"
Oh, Sadie, Oh, Sadie, Sadie:
Trumps ever on for the bizarre.

This claim Melania did douse,
Noting who resides in White House.
"Definitely first…" Ivana—
Book publicity nirvana.
We ask: Who'd want to claim the louse.

Here in inventory monger,
Wife twenty-seven years younger.
Former model of lingerie,
One day subject to age ennui,
But now there's still clichéd hunger.

I have known Paris Hilton for much of her young life and have always recognized her as a great beauty. What people don't know is that she is a great beauty on the inside as well.—Donald Trump, blurb for *Confessions of an Heiress: A Tongue-in-Chic Peek Behind the Pose* by Paris Hilton (2004).

Trump had signed Hilton with Trump Model Management in the early 2000s. Paris' grandfather is Barron Hilton, a name Trump likes a lot.

I was on location doing a movie, and he called me right after he had gotten a divorce [from Marla Maples] and said, 'I really think we should date because you're America's sweetheart and I'm America's richest man and people would love it.'
—Brooke Shields, "Watch What Happens Live with Andy Cohen," Oct. 3, 2017

Ivana said she still talks with President Trump regularly but doesn't call the White House directly in order to avoid making first lady Melania Trump jealous. Ivana even referred to herself as the real "first Lady." I don't want to cause any kind of jealousy or something like that because I'm basically first Trump wife, OK? I'm first lady.
—Interview with Amy Robach, ABC News, Oct. 8 2017

Sixteen years ago, we profiled Donald Trump's then-girlfriend Melania Knauss. In our naked profile shoot on his customized Boeing 727 wearing handcuffs, wielding diamonds and holding a chrome pistol… Headline read: "Sex at 30,000 feet. Melania Knauss earns her air miles."
—*British GQ*, Nov. 8, 2016

[I]n early versions of Melania's official White House biography she listed the *GQ* cover among those she had "graced" as a model.
—Anna Nemtsova, Daily Beast, Sept. 5, 2018

[A]llies of Ted Cruz posted a photo from a shoot for a 2000 issue of *British GQ* in which a naked Melania is lying on her stomach on a white bearskin rug. "Meet Melania Trump. Your next First Lady," read the ad… Trump Tweeted, "My wife is hotter."
—Julia Joffe, *GQ,* April 27, 2016

For glossy magazine display
Featuring a public feast day,
Melania posed nude on bearskin.
What to say but "Chinney-chin-chin!"
For Trump, this was one more D-Day.

Here's more wisdom that Trump offers
From his very well-stocked coffers:
"What is thirty-five? Check-out time."
This is enzyme of total slime;
Plug up his mouth with a saucer.

Age 59, with pregnant wife,
Invaded by mental loosestrife,
Caught on hot mic with words so coarse.
Showing libido in full force
With techniques showing style of life.

There's that other event adverse.
With porn star getting a big purse
For silence about escapade
That should be termed a sexcapade.
Decades of Trump morals inverse.

But Trump's base fears not such foibles;
The Donald still viewed as royal.
Despite the mountains of great sleaze,
No scandal thwarts his devotees.
Evangelicals stay loyal.

Just fueled to keep Hillary out,
They weren't looking for a Boy Scout.
Sex acts won't keep him from heaven.
God, they say, gives mercy leaven.
So give three cheers for Trump redoubt.

Trumptide

He's quick to carry every grudge;
The Donald does like slinging sludge.
While posturing as a heartthrob,
He tags women fat pigs and slobs.
He's in need of psycho line-judge.

I'm automatically attracted to beautiful women—I just start kissing them. It's like a magnet... I don't even wait. And when you're a star, they let you do it. You can do anything. Grab them by the pussy. You can do anything.
—Donald Trump to "Access Hollywood's" Billy Bush, September 2005

Men at times talk like that.
—Rudy Giuliani to Jake Tapper, CNN, Oct. 9, 2016

Russian Twitter trolls deflected public attention from Trump's *Access Hollywood* story. Tweeting, "MSM (the mainstream media) is at it again with Billy Bush recording…What about telling Americans how Hillary defended a rapist and later laughed at his victim?"—Ryan Nakashima & Barbara Ortutay, AP, Nov. 20, 2017

We do know he had a one-night stand with Stormy Daniels when his fifth child by his third wife was four months old.
—Elizabeth Burke, Clyde Fitch Report, May 7, 2018

A lawyer for President Donald Trump arranged a $120,000 payment to a former adult-film star a month before the 2016 election as part of an agreement that precluded her from publicly discussing an alleged sexual encounter with Mr. Trump.—Michael Rothfeld & Joe Palazzolo, *Wall Street Journal*, Jan. 12, 2018

[In] another nondisclosure agreement involving an affair between an adult entertainer and a client of Cohen's, the NDA employed the pseudonyms… used in the Stormy Daniels NDA…Dennison agreed to pay Peterson $1.6 million, in exchange for Peterson's promise not to reveal the affair or her claim that Dennison had impregnated her…Payments were also delivered through Essential Consultants LLC, the same LLC created by Cohen to facilitate payment in the Stormy Daniels deal.—Paul Campos, *New York* Daily Intelligencer, May 8, 2018

They broke into the office of one of my personal attorneys, a good man….It's a real disgrace. It's an attack on our country in a true sense.—Donald Trump in Greg Miller, *The Apprentice* (2018)

Trump retained the party's base, particularly among religious voters (the three times married "pussy-grabber" won more than 80% of white evangelicals).—David Edgar, *The Guardian*, Nov. 23, 2017

In debates, out came the slam bat:
"That face! Who would vote for that?"
Attacks 'fat, ugly face' and 'slob,'
And rolls along with hatchet jobs.
Past time to bell this mangy cat.

We watched appalling candidate
All truth and ethics abnegate.
When he called woman a fat pig,
His ever faithful danced a jig,
Their fine hero to adulate.

Megyn Kelly asked tough question;
Candidate Trump retched aggression;
"Blood coming out of her eyes...
Out of her whatever," he slides.
The man rejects all discretion.

Now he screams of media blight;
He once cared not about their cites.
"As long as you've got beautiful
Piece of ass." Trump as usual,
Putting horniness in floodlight.

But Trump goes beyond words feral;
Actions put women in peril.
There's a long list of accusers
Pointing to him as abuser—
With a moral code that's sterile.

Of those citing Trump's actions crude,
He warned, "These liars will be sued."
Such threat is classic polemic
To shield bad conduct pandemic.
Creepiness factor multitude.

Press Sec Sanders:"He has spoken."
Her rebuttal worse than hokum.
She offers degraded Fake News:
Official, functionary ruse.
In truth, Trump isn't house-broken.

Trump's [24] accusers have tellingly similar stories: he kissed them, he groped them, he leered at them... He also did all of this in familiar surroundings—as if the women were merely part of the buildings and organizations that he owned.
—Jia Tolentino, *The New Yorker*, Oct. 20, 2016

Megyn Kelly... You've called women you don't like 'fat pigs,' 'dogs,' 'slobs,' and 'disgusting animals.'
Trump: Only Rosie O'Donnell.
—GOP debate, August 2015

I have tremendous respect for woman and the many roles they serve that are vital to the fabric of our nation.
—@realDonaldTrump, Twitter, March 8, 2017

Please, please think about this. If you found that your twisted neighbor was tweeting out such insane diatribes against females, you'd not just notify Twitter, but you'd call the cops to protect yourself and your family against the neighborhood freak.
—Linda Stozi, *New York Daily News*, June 29, 2017

As the First Lady has stated publicly, when her husband gets attacked he will punch back 20 times harder.
—Stephanie Grisham, Press Secretary to Melania Trump, June 2017

Trump has indulged in more scandalous behavior than is easy to recount. For some reason, his record of misogyny, in both language and acts, his running compendium of self-satisfied creepiness, the accumulated complaints against him of sexual harassment and assault (all denied, of course), have attracted only modest attention, one defamation lawsuit, and no congressional interest.
—David Remnick, *The New Yorker*, Nov. 20, 2017

The feds have agreed to not prosecute the corporate owner of the *National Enquirer* over a $150,000 deal struck shortly before the 2016 election that silenced a former Playboy model who claims to have had a long-running affair with President Trump...
  —Kaja Whitehouse and Bruce Golding, *New York Post*, Dec. 12, 2018

He has spoken. What an affront.
Nothing better than a pig's grunt.
Lacking any moral ground floor.
We must locate a moral core.
Time to mount ethics battlefront.

Yes, the President has spoken,
With message leaving us chokin'.
Stop the ceaseless infomercial
Manifesting ethics servile.
We see a White House that's smokin'.

Has spoken: assaulter-in-chief,
With women as aperitif.
Turpitude reprehensible
Totally indefensible.
Remove the polity fig leaf.

The prez has spoken, rude and crass,
We sit here without safety glass.
Daily assaults of verbal puss,
Harm each and every one of us.
We must stop this prolonged trespass.

The prez speaks & speaks some more:
His preferred timbre is a roar.
The president, he does yammer
With his loud, soul-breaking clamor
And his twisted esprit de corps.

Yes, the president has spoken.
Yes, the president has spoken.
Huckabee Sanders does repeat
As though she were just shooting skeet.
Long since, this record got broken.

"Has spoken": favored non-reply,
Treating the press like tsetse fly.
Yawp! The president has spoken.
Yuk! The president has spoken.
Time for us to answer: BYE-BYE!

Question: At least 16 women accused the president of sexually harassing them throughout the course of the campaign. Last week, during a press conference in the Rose Garden, the President called these accusations 'fake news.' Is the official White House position that all of these women are lying?
Sarah Huckabee Sanders: Yeah, we've been clear on that from the beginning, and the President has spoken on it.
—White House briefing, Oct. 27, 2017

*"The president has spoken on it.—Sarah Huckabee Sanders, Oct. 27, 2017
*Look, as the president said himself.—Sarah Huckabee Sanders, Dec. 11, 2017
*He stated several times.—Sarah Huckabee Sanders, Feb. 20, 2018
*We speak on behalf of the president, day in, day out.
—Sarah Huckabee Sanders, April 6, 2018
*[T]he president has spoken about that.—Sarah Huckabee Sanders, May 11, 2018
* I'm here to speak on behalf of the president. He's made his comments clear.
—Sarah Huckabee Sanders, Aug. 7, 2018

You guys need to take a step back…and quit going after the Trump administration on every little thing that takes place.
—Sarah Huckabee Sanders, July 18, 2018

Almost everyone agrees that my Administration has done more in less than two years than any other Administration in the history of our Country …
— (@realDonaldTrump), Twitter, Sept. 5, 2018

What I see coming out of this building is pure and total success. He's had the most successful two years of any president in modern history.
—Sarah Huckabee Sanders, "ABC Good Morning America," Sept. 5, 2018

More and more, Sanders presents a televised reënactment of Trump's Twitter feed…Sanders often appears to mistake journalism for stenography or cheerleading.
—Paige Williams, *The New Yorker*, Sept. 24, 2018

God "wanted Donald Trump to become president."
—Sarah Huckabee Sanders, Christian Broadcasting Network, Jan. 30, 2019

We must not succumb to the bleak,
But prompt plans for redress must seek.
Time to send the president home—
With his girls, his tweets, and his comb.
Let the Constitution plain speak.

Read Article 1, Section 9:
Foreign emoluments align.
Sorry, this is not about sex,
But speaks to The Donald's apex:
The foreign connections goldmine.

We need regime morality
Based on rules of legality.
Off with ego, bedlam, and greed.
Rules of order are what to heed,
Out with blaring venality.

Read Constitution conditions
And then let's go for abscission;
Impeach
The leech.
End Oval Office vendition.

Follow Jefferson, we beseech:
Impeach. Impeach. Impeach. Impeach.
Hear. Hear.
Our Constitution is quite clear,
Our remedy is within reach.

"Trump's Emoluments Trap." It is our constitutional duty to protect our citizens from the harms Mr. Trump is causing by his violation of the Constitution—and to help safeguard our country from undue influences, foreign and domestic.
—Karl A. Racine, attorney general for the District of Columbia
Brian F. Frosh, attorney general for Maryland
Normal I. Eisen, chairman of Citizens for Responsibility and Ethics in Washington
New York Times, July 27, 2018

Make yourself heard—for every voice counts!
—*Dr. Seuss, Horton Hears a Who!* (1954)

Then act now. Go! Don't leave it to others.
—Sophocles, *Antigone* (ca. 441 BC)

IV TRUMPETERRING:
The Merchandizing Family

The Donald

Selling himself as a kingpin,
Trump is not a Trumpelstiltskin.
The Donald likes to crow and crow:
Things with his name always make dough.
He is a man without chagrin.

For his project on the Hyatt,
Trump mob hires caused much disquiet:
Concrete contractors, wrecking crew,
And the carpenters union, too.
Even newsstand Roy Cohn striate.

Football team buy gave Trump real fame
In the national news main frame.
Sports Illustrated big attention:
New York Times pumped up ascension.
Trump a whiz at media game.

Now foreign vendors pay big bucks,
Making the Trump name run amok:
Vodka and ties carry Trump brand.
Trump Home Collection®: on demand,
Tables and ottomans deluxe.

Suits from China and Mexico
Trump offers as success "Hello."
Buy at Amazon or e-Bay
And feel part of Trump passion play—
Or maybe on a TV show.

Trump once sold steaks really quite thick;
And Success deodorant stick.
 "I'm Back & You're Fired" not success,
But faux coat of arms does impress
Supporters enthralled with his shtick.

I want five children, like in my own family because with five, then I know that one will be guaranteed to turn out like me.—Donald J. Trump, in Marie Brenner, *Vanity Fair*, September 1990

With his father's financial backing and political connections, young Donald [turned] the broken down Commodore hotel next to Grand Central Station into the Grand Hyatt. The amazing part was…the way City Hall poured taxpayer money into Trump's pockets.
—David Cay Johnston, *Temples of Chance: How America Inc. Bought Out Murder Inc to Win Control of the Casino Business* (1992)

Instead of the promised promotional work for cheerleaders, [Trump's team] arranged appearances in local bars. "I really don't feel that going into bars in these skimpy outfits in front of 25 drunken men is the kind of publicity we should be involved in," said Madeline Coangelo, squad director.
—Robert McG. Thomas Jr., *New York Times*, April 20, 1984

Success by Trump Eau de Toilette Spray: Was $60, now $30.

Success by Trump Deodorant Stick: Was $14, Now $2.99

Trump rump, I mean Trump Steak, debuted this week on my home shopping channel. Finally a place to get filet mignon for only $96 per pound.
—Kristi O'Harran, Herald.Net, June 7, 2007

Trump barstools for sale in Dubai,
Alcohol banned? Cash is ally.
Home Galleries beds and love seats,
All with Trump parvenu conceit:
Has wares for every by and by.

Trump offers much more to consume:
Cuff links, pillows, and some perfume.
Spring water, mattress, and eye wear.
Not known is franchise for The Hair,
Which sits there, a unique orange bloom.

Vitamins The Donald once sold.
For better health, people were told.
Sent out pills from a urine test,
Parcels showed Trump Family crest.
Never say this guy isn't bold.

His Network bought Ideal Health brand,
A pyramid scheme, oh so grand:
$139.95 for The Test & month's supply.
Products that science does decry.
And then Trump did the line expand.

There's the deal in Azerbaijan:
Truly venal booty can-can.
Ivanka bragged of role massive.
Trump mouthpiece says his was passive.
Foreign Corrupt Practices Act—WHAM!

Trump defines self as branding shark,
Seventy-seven China marks:
Bars and management consulting.
Anywhere or time: fees pulsing.
Trump: The Name-for-Sale oligarch.

Golf clubs, escort services, spas:
Hello, there, Emolument Clause.
Trump's China trademarks do increase.
The Constitution says: "Surcease!
But Trump just shouts his Ha Ha Has.

The Trump Network's losers were not Donald Trump, but mainly the more than 21,000 people who invested in the company as recruiters, hoping to make it big, swayed entirely by Donald Trump's promises.—Ian Tuttle, "Add another Yuge Failure to Trump's Pile: The Trump Network," *National Review*, March 8, 2016

Trump has made a lot of money doing deals with businesspeople from the former Soviet Union, and at some of these deals bear many of the warning signs of money laundering and other financial crimes. Deals in Toronto, Panama, New York, and Miami involved money from sources in the former Soviet Union who hid their identities through shell companies and exhibited other indications of money laundering.
—Adam Davidson, *The New Yorker*, July 19, 2018

The President helped build a hotel in Azerbaijan that appears to be a corrupt operation engineered by oligarchs tied to Iran's Revolutionary Guard.
—Adam Davidson, *The New Yorker*, March 13, 2017

Once upon a time—long before The Apprentice and the golf courses and the TRUMP-branded-underwear-vodka-mattresses-steaks-wine-and-who-knows-what-else and the questionable online education venture and the choreographed wrestling farces and the skyscrapers and the sprawling casinos and the boxing matches and the magazine covers and the beauty pageants and the fisticuffs with City Hall and the serial bankruptcies….
—Timothy L. O'Brien, *TrumpNation: The Art of Being The Donald* (2005)

Federal and state investigators are scrutinizing the employment documents of immigrants without legal status who said they worked at President Trump's golf club in New Jersey…fake green cards and social Security numbers that supervisors at the golf club provided.
—Emily Wax-Thibodeau, *Washington Post*, Dec. 29, 2018

Ivana

Wanting credit she says is due,
Ivana wrote book of how-to:
Raise kids and also make big bucks
Selling lots of items deluxe.
With kids, a stress on follow-through.

Note: Kids have to be in college
Ere Donald does verbal haulage.
That's when he can talk big business
And apparently find fitness.
The Donald does not schmooze smallage.

She flew first class with kids in coach;
Not listening when pleas they broached,
Stressing kids need to earn the bread
In order to move on ahead.
Until then, they mustn't encroach.

Ivana calls Ivanka "star";
She's a woman who will go far.
Writing a benedictory,
Lauds daughter with Dad's victory
And predicts future *Wunderbar!*

Melania

There's Melania™ Jewelry.
Under $200, so no worry
About buying self a nice gift.
She offered beauty at such thrift.
White House sell went topsy-turvy.

Schlepped valise of baubles to schmooze
For feature on Fox Business News.
"Really beautiful plastic" watch
In four different colors: topnotch.
These bargain pieces should enthuse.

Inspired by New York and Palm Beach,
Luxe "within every woman's reach."
Her own wear from different bracket:
$51,500 Dolce & Gabana jacket.
But on Fox, low-cost she did preach.

T]he credit for raising such great kids belongs to me. I made the decisions about their education, activities, travel, childcare, and allowances. When each one finished college, I said to my ex-husband, "Here is the finished product. Now it's your turn…" I made tens of millions selling House of Ivana clothes, fragrances, and jewelry on HSN Tampa, QVC London, and TSC Canada.
—Ivana Trump, *Raising Trump* (2017)

[H]e does not know how to make small talk and he certainly was not going to say, 'Oh, choo, choo, choo, choo. How cute we are today. Let's go to the park in the stroller.' No. That was not his kind of thing. He only started talking to them when they were in university and they could talk business.—Ivana Trump to Michael Riedel, *New York Post*, Oct. 9, 2017

"Are you still a believer in Santa? 'Cause at 7, it's marginal, right?"—Donald Trump to 7-year-old who called NORAD government Santa tracking program. Dec. 2018

Ivana Haute Couture Fragrances
Courageously Feminine…Irresistibly Romantic…
original fragrance, pink label, pink box.

White House website touts Melania Trump's modeling and jewelry line.
—Kelsey Snell, *Washington Post*, Jan. 30, 2017

The first lady earned six figures from an agreement with Getty images that paid royalties to the Trumps and mandated that photos be used in positive coverage. Yahoo News, NBC News, *Marie Claire, the Daily Mail*, My San Antonio, *Houston Chronicle, House Beautiful*, and SF Gate… are among those that have featured Melania's highly stylized family portraits since Trump took office.
—NBC News, July 2, 2018

Melania donned a white pith helmet on her solo trip through Africa, a colonialist staple of British soldiers on the continent in the 19th century. After wearing the symbol of colonial oppression, she declared in an interview, "I could say I'm the most bullied person on the world."—Matt Stieb and Britina Cheng, *New York* Intelligencer, Dec. 31, 2018

The Trumpkins

Special Assist to President,
Ivanka's West Wing resident.
There is no need for a caucus:
Ivanka has White House office,
On hand Dad's regime to augment.

Just for the tab of her book's price,
Fashionista gives life advice:
"Nothing's ever handed to you,"
So let's just stop all that boo-hoo
From those not rolling in edelweiss.

With her self-success she bombards:
First book was titled *The Trump Card*.
"Apprentice" special two-hour blitz
Showcased lots of Ivanka glitz.
In realpolitik, Dad's vanguard.

Has quite a career with her brand:
$100 million a year she commands.
Stuff made in China: without fuss;
Worker protection? Not discussed.
Macy's to Walmart, goods on hand.

$62.97 has the Trump feel:
The metallic sheath: quite a deal.
Woven diamond bracelet: high price,
Silvertone zinc cast might suffice.
At low cost, it carries Trump seal.

Those who for Trump diamonds aspire
Find that lots of cash they require.
But there's also that fine fettle:
Imitation Rhodium-Plated White Metal,
Not priced for financial quagmire.

For $32.47, Eau de Parfum spray,
Hurrah! Box made in USA!
Tummy Control Pants and shampoo—
Nothing seems beyond her purview.
Maybe next we'll see Trump® toupee.

Don't go out of your way to correct a false assumption if it plays to your advantage.—Ivanka Trump, *The Trump Card: Playng to Win in Work and Life* (2009)

Shop Ivanka's look from her #RNC speech
—@IvankaTrump, Twitter, July 22, 2015

White House as QVC [flagship shopping channel]. It has started.
—@EricLiptonNYT, Twitter, Nov. 15, 2016

Ivanka Danka-Doo is America's youngest First Lady. I know, technically she's not the First Lady, but she is the only woman related to Donald Trump who has an office in the West Wing. His actual wife has an office on QVC.
—Joy Behar, *The Great Gasbag: An A-to-Z Study Guide to Surviving Trump World* (2017)

Ivanka Trump is…more a logo than a person, a scarecrow stuffed with branding, an heiress-turned model-turned-multimillionaire's-wife playacting as an authority on the challenges facing working women so that she can sell more pastel sheath dresses.
—Lindy West, *New York Times*, Sept. 6, 2017

It was a pasteboard "C-suite" feminist look—pastel-toned sheath dresses, structured bags conjuring Céline or Prada, but often made of vinyl, pumps and flats that closely imitated higher-end shoes… watered-down simulacra of luxury goods, accessibly priced, elite-seeming but poorly made.
—Rhoda Garelick, *New York Times*, July 26, 2018

China this month awarded Ivanka Trump seven new trademarks across a broad collection of businesses, including books, housewares and cushions.
—Sui-Lee Wee, *New York Times*, May 28, 2018

Trump had called for more support for working women around the world, but she has remained silent about the largely female garment workforce in Asian countries that makes her clothing. Her brand…has declined to identify the factories that produce her goods or detail how the workers are treated or paid.
—Drew Harwell, Annie Gowten, & Swati Gupta, *Washington Post*, Nov. 26, 2017

When The Daughter spoke on news show,
Press release: Fans could follow glow
And make a fine Trump connection:
$10,000 in Jewelry Collection.
Family motto is "Go! Go! Go!"

Kellyanne Conway criticized
For telling Fox News what she prized.
Urging, "Go buy Ivanka's stuff!"
Trumpsters can never buy enough.
Trump-buy is ever canonized.

Never you mind, never you mind.
For a much much bigger design:
Ivanka Trump Marks LLC
With products there in ten countries.
For money this Trumpette is primed.

Each Kushner picks up a steak knife
With the China prez and his wife.
Ivanka snaps up three trademarks,
Just adding to her branded arc.
Here we see how the Trumps contrive.

Hubby had arranged this meeting
For the Mar-a-Lago greetings.
Spa services, jewelry, and bags
Now on the Chinese Trumpette flag,
Just one more deal they're completing.

Tweets love for blue collar workforce
When in truth she's China clotheshorse.
Ivanka's world is meet and greet,
For future use on a spreadsheet,
On Labor, she needs basic course.

She is a chip off the old block,
Quite deep in The Donald bedrock.
She has the talent Dad hoped for:
Rapacious huckster top drawer.
Fitting heir to cock of the walk.

A "fashion alert" was initially sent to journalists by Monica Marder, vice president of sales for Ivanka Trump Fine Jewelry. It promoted Ivanka as wearing "her favorite bangle from the Metropolis Collection" [on "60 Minutes"]. The bracelet costs $8,800 to $10,000. "Please share this with your clients…" the email said.
—NBC News, Nov. 15, 2017

Ivanka Trump Marks LLC, which handles her trademarks, is continuing to push into unexplored commercial spaces bearing her name…And the Trump Organization's hotels in Washington and Vancouver each operate a trademarked Spa by Ivanka Trump.
—Bloomberg, Aug. 10, 2017

Ivanka Trump Marks LLC includes: Leather And Imitations Of Leather, And Goods Made Of These Materials And Not Included In Other Classes; Animal Skins, Hides; Trunks And Traveling Bags; Umbrellas, Parasols And Walking Sticks; Whips, Harness And Saddlery.
—Bizapedia, Updated April 8, 2018

Ivanka Trump's particular strain of fast fashion outfits for Women Who Work (which she made into a hashtag) never made sense. Not only were the clothes often hideous, they never seemed aimed at women who would intentionally spend money on a Trump brand, and young women in need of inexpensive professional outfits have a wide range of other options.
—Meredith Clark, NBC News, July 24, 2018

Felix Sater [Russian-born businessman], who sometimes carried a business card identifying him as a "senior adviser" to Mr. Trump, pursued Russian deals throughout the 2000s. On one visit in which he was accompanied by Donald Trump Jr. and Ivanka Trump, he arranged for Ms. Trump to sit in Mr. Putin's chair during a tour of the Kremlin.—Mike McIntire, Megan Twohey & Mark Mazzetti, *New York Times*, Nov. 29, 2018

"I'm the first daughter."—Ivanka to Steve Bannon, in Bob Woodward, *Fear: Trump in the White House* (2018)

Junior

Veep of The Organization,
With money grab dedication.
Branding, marketing, ops and sales.
Bombast with no probity scales—
Just Trump money elevation.

Gave fine "Apprentice" description:
"Informational" prescription.
Jr, filled airways with Trump schemes,
Getting applause for vulgar themes,
Older son needs no audition.

For Kremlin link he opened door
Bringing Kushner and Manafort.
Dad named it adoption impasse;
People see a snake in the grass—
And something else under the floor.

Showing a lack of much credo,
He got the nickname of Fredo,
For shooting himself in the foot.
In explanations he's hard put
To flee the coming tornado.

Joins with D'Souza on far right,
Pardoned by Dad from felon bite.
Connect with gauge sidereal:
Film pitched Hitler as liberal.
Looks like a case of bad brain blight.

At *Enquirer*, he's truth teller.
This paper, once a big seller,
Says when Dems tried to do damage,
Junior did bring in the salvage:
News from an Alt Facts propeller.

This fine *Enquirer* insider
Says Russia link fake divider:
Hillary plot; FBI moles,
Ever digging subversive holes,
Junior as truth dispatch rider.

Donald Trump Jr. spent more time in Moscow than his father—flying in repeatedly from 2006 onward…He was meant to oversee Dad's Moscow tower…
June 3, 2016 email was unequivocal. The Russian government was offering Trump damaging material on Clinton as part of its efforts to make Trump president.
—Luke Harding, *Collusion: Secret Meetings, Dirty Money, and How Russia Helped Donald Trump Win* (2017)

A Russian lawyer who met with President Donald Trump's oldest son last year says he indicated a law targeting Russia could be re-examined if his father won the election and asked her for written evidence that illegal proceeds went to Hillary Clinton's campaign.
—Irina Reznik & Henry Meyer, Bloomberg, Nov. 6, 2017

[Donald] Trump personally dictated a statement… in Trump Jr.'s name saying that the participants in the Trump Tower meeting had "primarily discussed a program about the adoption of Russian children."
—Greg Miller, *The Apprentice* (2018)

Mr. Trump accepted a ring from the Bailey Banks & Biddle jewelry store in exchange for publicity, recreating his proposal at its Short Hills Mall location in New Jersey… Headline in the *New York Post:* "Trump Jr. Is the Cheapest Gazillionaire: Heirhead Proposes With Free 100G Ring."
—Laura M. Holson, *New York Times*, March 18, 2017

Excited to cohost the DC red carpet premiere of @DineshD'Souza new movie Death of a Nation tomorrow. It's going to fire up Republicans for the midterms exploring how fascism so closely links to the platform of the progressive left today. WATCH IT!
—@DonaldJTrumpJr, Twitter, July 31, 2018

In "Death of a Nation," Dinesh D'Souza is no longer preaching to the choir, he's preaching to the mentally unsound.—Owen Gleiberman, *Variety*, July 31, 2018

FBI PLOT TO IMPEACH TRUMP! The rogue agents, Obama & Hillary's role and what Donald Jr. is doing to stop it… Behind the scenes, Donald Jr. has diligently blueprinted the chilling coup attempt…The president plans to grind these traitors to democracy into dust.
—*National Enquirer* cover story, Jan. 8, 2018

For first Prez endorsement ever,
Enquirer pulled the Trump lever.
CEO needs Saudi flexion;
Trump gave White House intersection.
Buddies sweeping dirt together.

Junior's new object of selling:
Girlfriend affirms he's compelling.
Gilfoyle, given a Fox News smack,
Sings at Trump 2020 PAC
And does Junior's course rappelling.

This girlfriend shines in the spotlight
While five kids face family blight.
Yes, Junior is much like his Dad:
Liking role as marriage nomad.
It's part of his Trumpster birthright.

Eric

Does golf clubs Colts Neck to Dubai.
Nineteen clubs with Trump glut to buy.
Golf, tennis, weddings, and fitness,
Ever test consumer litmus.
Eager with Trump brand to supply.

Fetes: "luminous votive candles"
And all else the purse can handle.
Wedding cost at Trump Winery:
$31,000 for 100 guests' finery.
In Trump aura they can amble.

Using Jefferson quotes as bait
To lure client through Wine Club gate.
This promise is offered erstwhile:
"The unparalleled Trump lifestyle"—
Four bottles will bring luxe au fait.

Eric's Foundation fund events;
Trump golf club collected the rents.
The Donald was sure to get paid
Before charity made the grade.
Charity starts at home—Trump tent.

Wooing Saudi Business, Tabloid Mogul Had a Powerful Friend: Trump.—Jim Rutenberg, Kate Kelly, Jessica Silver-Greenberg, & Mike McIntire, *New York Times* headline, March 29, 2018

I've seen him [Donald Jr] at these political rallies. He commands the room. He's a compelling political figure…he's incredibly bright…number one political figure on the right.—Kimberly Gilfoyle <u>in</u> Sean Moran, Breitbart News Daily, July 6, 2018

I am thrilled to be joining Don Jr. across the country in amplifying the America-first message. We…make the perfect team.—Kimberly Gilfoyle, in Richard Johnson, *New York Post*, Page Six, Aug. 27, 2018

The Trump Winery in Charlottesville, Va., is hoping to hire farmworkers and laborers to tend to the property's crops, nursery and greenhouse. The jobs would start March 19…. The pay rate is $11.46 per hour…The request was filed through the H-2A visa program.
—Brett Samuels, *The Hill*, Jan. 18, 2018

The FBI and the New Jersey Attorney General's Office are investigating allegations that the Trump National Golf Club provided undocumented immigrant employees with fake social security cards and green cards.
—Andrew Denney, The Inquisitr, Dec. 29, 2018

A room at Albemarle Estate Trump Winery, Charlottesville: $599 per night—plus taxes and fees. Full stay deposit is required at time of booking. Cancellations made within 30 days prior day of arrival will be assessed a cancellation penalty of 100 percent of stay.
—Information from website

Russia has never tried to use leverage over me.
I HAVE NOTHING TO DO WITH RUSSIA - NO DEALS, NO LOANS, NO NOTHING!
—@realDonaldTrump, Twitter, Jan. 11, 2017

We have all the funding we need out of Russia. We've got some guys that really, really love golf, and they're really invested in our programs. We just go there all the time.
—Eric Trump to golf journalist James Dodson, in Bill Littlefield, "Only a Game," May 5, 2017

Wife is media go-getter:
Tweets with political fester.
Trusty part of the Trump stable,
She's part of White House Round Table,
Conflict-of-interest bestir.

With her access to White House knobs,
Her relatives also get jobs.
Government sinecures deployed,
Trump rolled-out kin fully employed.
We get Trump translation of Nobs.

Eric and Lara share Dad's Tweets:
"America great again" bleats.
Trump gene for sticking to greed line
Puts armor around any spine:
Just The Donald heat and repeat.

Jared

High school grades were not so stellar
Daddy's money was compeller.
Harvard entrance came with Dad's zeal
For paying out big money deal.
He'll never be a cave dweller.

He who dislikes pagination;
Brought newspaper to negation.
Having no insight to Grub Street,
Jared grabbed hold the catbird seat:
The Observer saw stagnation.

Jersey slumlord to all things State,
Kushner always nearby home plate.
Sis Nicole hawked wares in Beijing
To profit in a visa scheme.
Post-vote divestments: fifty-eight.

Value's set by those he owes dough:
No, not Larry, Curly, and Moe;
Blackstone/Citigroup connections;
And Deutsche Bank redirection,
Vnescheconombank is there also.

Lara Trump, the face of her father-in-law's re-election campaign, has been hosting high-level meetings within the White House to push a variety of domestic policy initiatives, a clear crossing of the well-established line between campaign work and public service, ethics, and government watchdogs told *Newsweek*. "This White House is being run like a family business, and campaigning is their bread and butter," said David Gergen, a presidential adviser who has served in four White House administrations.
—Chris Riotta, *Newsweek*, Nov. 3, 2017

Lara's brother, Kyle Yunaska, named chief of staff at Energy Department Office of Energy Policy…He participated in 2013 in a competition to find the "hottest bachelors" in Washington, D.C.
—Josh Delk, *The Hill*, Nov. 8, 2017

[My book, *The Price of Admission: How America's Ruling Class Buys Its Way into Elite Colleges*—and Who Gets Left Outside the Gates] reported that New Jersey real estate developer Charles Kushner had pledged $2.5 million to Harvard University…not long before his son Jared was admitted to the prestigious Ivy League school…I also quoted administrators at Jared's high school, who described him as a less than stellar student and expressed dismay at Harvard's decision.
—Daniel Golden, *ProPublica*, Nov. 28, 2016

It's unclear if Jared Kushner ever really read The *Observer* before he bought it. –Rich Cohen, *Vanity Fair*, Nov. 2017

A much-criticized visa program that allows foreigners to win fast-track immigration in return for investing $500,000 in U.S. properties was extended in a bill signed by President Trump just one day before a sister of senior White House advisor Jared Kushner pitched the program to Chinese investors.—Michael Kranish, *Washington Post*, May 7, 2017

The concern about Deutsche Bank is that they have a history of laundering Russian money…And this, apparently, was the one bank that was willing to do business with the Trump Organization.
—Rep. Adam Schiff, Meet the Press, Dec. 16, 2018

Yes, he owes a zillion big bucks.
There's IDB Bank deal deluxe,
Apollo, Goldman and the rest.
Bank of Scotland refused press quests—
Waiting for The Princeling's efflux.

In charge of Middle East peace deal,
Kushner to Israel does kneel,
With Bet El not wasting their time
Cashing in on Trump actions prime:
 "God gave it to us" glockenspiel.

Plenty of intimate conclaves.
Made Jared a real Saudi fave.
Forging Oval Office platform,
They fed him all their hawkish norms
And built the White House Saudi nave.

Long seeing Jared as a puss,
Bannon tossed him close to the bus—
He delivered a sidewinder.
While loudmouthing a reminder:
This guy's a political klutz.

Bannon's out and Jared's still in.
At the White House to spin-spin-spin.
We see him here, we see him there,
We do see him everywhere:
He's still The Donald's caudal fin.

Famous meeting at Trump Tower
Was not to admire the flowers.
Claim of adoption dialogue
Did sound like the hair of the dog
While it looked liked Kremlin showers.

Jared, the meddling go-getter,
Does avoid action on Twitter.
So give three wholehearted cheers
For not echoing this Trump's sphere.
But he is a counterfeiter.

Kushner Cos owes hundreds of millions of dollars on a 41-story office building on Fifth Avenue…Over the past two years, executives and family members have sought substantial overseas investment from previously undisclosed places: South Korea's sovereign-wealth fund, France's richest man, Israeli banks and insurance companies, and exploratory talks with a Saudi developer.
—David Kocieniewski & Caleb Melby, Bloomberg, Aug. 31, 2017

As the [Khashoggi] killing set off a firestorm around the world and American intelligence agencies concluded that it was ordered by Prince Mohammed, Mr. Kushner became the prince's most important defender inside the White House…
—David D. Kirkpatrick, Ben Hubbard, Mark Landler & Mark Mazzetti, *New York Times*, Dec. 8, 2018

Mr. Kushner has expanded his portfolio into a far-ranging set of issues, including Middle East peace, the opiod epidemic, relations with China and Mexico and reorganizing the federal government from top to bottom. "Everything runs through me," he told corporate executives during the transition.
—Peter Baker, Glenn Thrush, & Maggie Haberman, *New York Times,* April 15, 2017

Jared is such a hidden genius that no one understands.
—Nikki Haley, announcing her resignation as United Nations ambassador, Oct. 9, 2018

The Kushner-Kislyak meeting…took place at Trump Tower. Michael Flynn was present, too. Kushner… asked Kislyak if it would be possible to set up a secret and secure communications channel between the Trump transition team and the Kremlin.—Luke Harding, *Collusion, Secret Meetings, Dirty Money, and How Russia Helped Donald Trump Win* (2017)

On state TV, Vladimir Zhirinovsky, the nationalist firebrand, had predicted that Trump would serve two full terms, followed by eight years of an Ivanka Trump presidency and eight more of Jared Kushner.
  —Greg Miller, *The Apprentice* (2018)

CODA

In Trumpocracy, there's no complication
In the lavishness of the family station.
Recognizing no moral clutter,
Just look to where the bread is buttered.
No chance of ethical resuscitation.

They seek gold here, they seek gold there;
All the Trumps seek it everywhere.
Is The Donald in heaven?
Is he in hell?
We only know he's a one-man cartel,
And the Constitution demands "Forswear!"

Trumpocracy offers huge complication
In the lavishness of its family station.
We mustn't parse over political clutter
As they grab for money all a-flutter.
Time now for Constitutional ablation.

Let's forgo the snipe hunts
And heed the emoluments.
Stop the hypocrisy!
Stand up for democracy!
We've got the Constitutional document.

Trump *ÜberAlles* offers legal breach
In its presidential greed overreach.
The Constitution offers solution
Without a citizens' revolution.
Use the Emoluments Clause to impeach.

Our Constitution should keep us straight.
Saving us from Oval Office freight.
With liberty and justice for all,
Make this The Year of The Trump fall.
All hail Article 1, Section 9, Clause 8.

It's our choices, Harry, that show what we truly are,
far more than our abilities.
—J. K. Rowling, *Harry Potter and the Chamber of Secrets* (2013)

If it was so, it might be; and if it were so, it would be, but as it isn't, it ain't.
—Lewis Carroll, *Through the Looking-Glass* (1872)

V BEDLAM:
Bouncing Along with the Cabinet

We've now got the Trumpolition
With lots of ethics abscission.
Each Trump Tweet brings one more shock
From White House orangey peacock
With short thumb on total fission.

This man coined the phrase,"you're fired!"
Causes retch when he says, "You're hired!"
Viewing his administration,
Gives us Yuge psych supperation,
Watching the "Me" ethos transpire.

Looking at the millionaire class
Dancing in Trump's cabinet chasse,
Recall that "Drain the Swamp!" slogan
Bursting from his campaign blow-gun.
Goldman-Sachs fills office morass.

Rule of, by, and for the 1%,
Vicious clan is in clout ascent.
Competing for class advantage,
The public weal they mismanage.
For high flyers, it's now Advent.

Let's start with Mister **Manafort**,
With talent in foreign cavort.
Post-Lewandowski, pre-Bannon;
Blown up by laundering cannon.
Now he's buried deeply in torts.

This set the tone for picks Trump makes
In the mammoth money sweepstakes.
A lawyer and a lobbyist
With behavior quite naughtiest.
Do secure him current headaches.

Look astern.
—Robert Lewis Stevenson, *Treasure Island* (1883)

Lincoln had a team of rivals, Trump has a team of Morons.
—Paul Krugman, Nobel Laureate, *New York Times*, Jan. 14, 2019

In opposition to the rabble of protesters trying to deter or destroy the president stands a stout wall of defenders who meet together weekly…to study the Bible, pray, and seek God's counsel for President Trump and his allies in the government. The meetings are known as the Trump Cabinet Bible Study, and most of the attendees are elected officials and cabinet officers who serve in the Trump administration, which has been called the most evangelical cabinet in history.
—Stephen E. Strang, *God and Donald Trump* (2017)

Trump's campaign chairman Paul Manafort had extensive, lucrative ties to Russia—and he lied about them. A lot.
—Hannah Levintova, *Mother Jones,* Dec. 29, 2017

[O]ne of the most preposterous meetings in modern politics: On June 9, 2016, Don Jr, Jared, and Paul Manafort met with a movie worthy cast of dubious characters in Trump Tower after having been promised damaging information about Hillary Clinton.
—Michael Wolf, *Fire and Fury: Inside the Trump White House* (2018)

Crocked loyalty to Trump required
To be part of Cabinet choir.
Experience for position
Not any part of the mission,
And so "The Swamp" is a quagmire.

Pix next to the Trump desk: Jackson;
It's not hard to see attraction
For this influence aspirant.
Lincoln: "Jackson reckless tyrant";
Trump drawn to the putrefaction.

Trump makes claim of the high I.Q.
Of his heyday management crew:
"Highest I.Q... ever assembled."
Ethos makes sane people tremble:
A rapacious billionaire brew.

Is this actually a brain trust?
Looks more like underbody rust—
Trump gave us a manure chancel,
Ever-ready for expansile.
And the sum total brings disgust.

Golf-plomacy is one strong key
For the presidential esprit.
During first 241 days in office
Seventy days in golf caucus.
Pax et Lux. More golf, less crappy.

The Wrecking Crew, zoo of grotesques,
Salute the Oval Office desk.
It's difficult to determine
Just who to call the worst vermin
In assembly of Kafkaesques.

After careful study intense,
One good thing about **Mike Pence**.
With cabinet posts in disrepair,
At least he has regular hair.
On barberage, he has defense.

A Complete Guide to All 17 (Known) Trump and Russia Investigations.
—Garret M. Graff, *Wired* headline, Dec. 17, 2018

Sometimes, part of making a deal is denigrating your competition.
— Donald J. Trump, *Trump: The Art of the Deal* (1987)

Lincoln ventured into politics as an ardent Whig, Characterizing the party as one founded to depose that "detestable, ignorant, reckless, vain, and malignant tyrant, Andrew Jackson."—Ron Chernow, *Grant* (2017)

Well, Andrew had a great history, and I think it's very rough when you take somebody off the bill.
—Donald J. Trump, NBC "Today," April 26, 2016

"The president has assembled the most talented cabinet in history and everyone continues to be dedicated towards advancing the president's American First agenda. Anything to the contrary is simply false and comes from unnamed sources who are either out of the loop or unwilling to turn the country around."—official White House statement to *New York Times*, Oct. 17, 2017

In Pence, Trump has found an obedient deputy whose willingness to suffer indignity and humiliation at the pleasure of the president appears boundless.
—McKay Coppins, *The Atlantic*, Jan/Feb 2018

As usual, Pence was staying out of the way. He didn't want to be tweeted about or called an idiot.—Bob Woodward, *Fear: Trump in the White House* (2018)

[E]vangelicals were doing spiritual cartwheels over the choice of Mike Pence. —David Brody & Scott Lamb, *The Faith of Donald J. Trump: A Spiritual Biography* (2018)

There is no human being who better personifies the unholy matrimony between the people who think America is a Christian nation and the people who think America is a corporate nation…Pence… a walking, squinting, nodding commitment to the GOP's base.
—Jason Sattler, *USA Today*, March 26, 2018

The cabinet, they do fumble
In accord with White House jumble.
"Blockhead," "knucklehead," and "moron";
There's no mention of "paragon."
They all continue to stumble.

Rex Tillerson, did sit at State,
Eagle Scout status on his plate.
Atlas Shrugged, his favorite book,
Capitalism was the hook
And shareholder cosmos his freight.

Putin gave Rex Russ anointment,
Then Donald made the appointment.
"Astonishing," were Rex oil deals,
Trump treated Rex as no big wheel,
Not noticing his deployment.

As part of the new White House strut,
Rex proposed 30% budget cut.
Wanting to show who the boss is:
Edicts come from Oval Office.
Career diplomats are just glut.

As try for slogan deflation,
North Korea conversation,
Rex met with Trump disapproval,
And even vicious accusal,
Causing call for Tweet cessation.

In his foreign travels afar,
Out of sync: Trump's tweets on Qatar.
"Not involved in how... he tweets,
When he tweets, why or, what he tweets."
For guidance, Rex had the North Star.

Through president's post on Twitter,
We learned Rexxon's now just litter.
How Rex got message pathetic;
No surprise from prex pyretic
Prideful as chaos emitter.

Asked by a reporter whether he had referred to Trump as a 'moron,' Tillerson did not deny the report but said that he 'wasn't going to deal with petty stuff like that.'
—*Boston Globe* news alert, Oct. 4, 2017

"I think it's fake news, but if he did that, I guess we'll have to compare IQ tests. And I can tell you who is going to win."
—Donald Trump to *Forbes*, Nov. 14, 2017

[Tillerson's] determined, prolonged efforts to pare down the state Department…have left the nation's leading diplomats shocked and demoralized, wandering around the silent halls past one empty office after another.—James Mason, *New York Review of Books*, Oct. 26, 2017

60 percent of career ambassadors have left the State Department since Trump took office.—Bethany Allen-Ebrihimian, *Foreign Policy*, Nov. 8, 2017

Asked about the massive number of vital diplomatic jobs that have remained vacant at the State Department as Rex Tillerson continues to systematically gut the agency, Trump said, "Let me tell you, the one that matters is me. I'm the only one that matters."
— Fox News, Nov. 2, 2017

State Department Under Secretary Steve Goldstein, Tillerson's de facto spokesman, released a statement Wednesday morning, saying Tillerson had not spoken to Mr. Trump and was unaware of the reason for his ouster. Goldstein was then subsequently fired by the administration.—CBS News, March 13, 2018

So often, the president would say here's what I want to do …and I would have to say to him, 'Mr. President… It violates the law. It violates treaty.'—Rex Tillerson, MD Cancer Center event, Houston, Dec. 6, 2018

He was the least lethal Secretary of State of my lifetime. Tiller was no Kissinger, Haig, Powell, Clinton or Albright and that was fine by me.—Jeffrey St. Clair, *Counterpunch*, March 16, 2018

Koch's **Pompeo** for Rex replace,
Leaves us without good will or grace.
He wants your full data info
To play his surveillance bingo,
Treating us as so much carcase.

Jefferson Beauregard Sessions III,
Att Gen, codes of conduct deferred,
Oh, those Russian conversations.
Rectitude in fluctuation,
Memory lapse beyond absurd.

He didn't lie, he did proclaim:
A poor memory is to blame
For not naming Russia contacts.
As well as schedule so jam-packed.
Does anyone believe con game?

Against immigration, each way,
He did our values deep betray.
Forsook Department of Justice
When Trump attacked with great fusses.
Ever there, Trump kudos to bray.

"Elf on shelf": Saturday Night Live,
Giving his stories a high five:
"I do not recall."
I do not recall."
Thus he did delay his crash dive.

Sessions was one more Eagle Scout.
On facts of justice, he struck out.
Heir of Rebel at Fort Sumter;
Himself: Bona fide destructor.
No more ethics than Brussels sprout.

Candidate Trump ripped hedge fund guys;
Now in his cabinet they fly.
Claimed "Getting away with murder,"
Just bombast from empty worder.
Now hedge fund friends are riding high.

One theory is that Kushner and Bannon wanted a weak Secretary of State so that they could run foreign policy out of the White House.— Jeffrey Toobin, *The New Yorker*, Sept. 10, 2018

Pompeo…is one of the largest benefactors of the pro-fossil-fuel Koch brothers on Capitol Hill.
—E&E News, Nov. 22, 2016

Mike Pompeo to replace Rex Tillerson as secretary of state puts a Koch favorite in charge of foreign policy.
—Adele M. Stan, prospect.org, March 14, 2018

Jeff Sessions, named after his father, named after his grandfather, named after Jefferson Davis, President of the Confederate States of America, and P.G.T. Beauregard, Confederate general who oversaw the bombardment of Fort Sumter.

In 1986, Pres. Ronald Reagan nominated Sessions, then a US attorney from Alabama, to be a federal judge. The Republican-controlled Senate rejected Mr. Sessions out of concern, based on devastating testimony by former colleagues, that he was a racist.—Editorial Board, *New York Times*, Nov. 18, 2016

In the Senate, Sessions was often Trump before Trump was Trump. He was an early advocate of a bigger, better, taller border fence.—Julia Ioffe, *Politico*, June 27, 2016

Sessions was the first member of the Senate to endorse Trump, and one year later he was confirmed by that body as US attorney general and head of the Department of Justice.
—Stephen E. Strang, *God and Donald Trump* (2017)

The government is dropping its case against the woman, a retired children's librarian, who laughed out loud during Attorney General Jeff Sessions' confirmation hearing.
—Laurel Walmsley, NPR, Nov. 8, 2017

The Russian Witch Hunt Hoax continues, all because Jeff Sessions didn't tell me he was going to recuse himself. I would have quickly picked someone else. So much time and money wasted, so many lives ruined…
@realDonaldTrump, Twitter, June 5, 2018

Steven Mnuchin, for Treasury,
Big bucks plenipotentiary.
Coming from Goldman Sachs riches,
Then dredging all hedge fund ditches,
Foreclosure king of misery.

Didn't disclose finances right—
Just $95 million oversight.
Cayman Islands funds all hush hush;
Congress OK came in a rush.
Corporate raiders get green light.

Here we have a real money hawk,
Use of government planes does shock.
Jetted out for total eclipse,
Saying he'd speak about tax tips
And check on the gold at Fort Knox.

Gary Cohn, Big Money alum,
Given a juicy White House plum,
Econ Council was his purview.
It's one more Goldman Sachs big coup,
From ready supply of pond scum.

Cohn took a salary onus;
With Goldman's $65 million parting bonus.
Cohn boasted sending jobs offshore,
To raise corporate profit score.
Money crisis: Goldman lowness.

Cohn bragged of what a thousand bucks
Will buy: A kitchen fix deluxe
Or whole lifestyle transformation.
The plan clearly obfuscation,
Based on mystery neutron flux.

Cohn replaced by **Larry Kudlow**,
He of money savvy pseudo.
Economics trends? Not a clue,
Farceur of trickle down voodoo,
Strumming on supply side banjo.

CREW requests copies of all records concerning authorization for and the costs of Treasury Secretary Steven Mnuchin's use of a government plane to travel to Lexington, Kentucky on Monday, August 21, accompanied by his wife Louise Linton.
—Citizens for Responsibility & Ethics in Washington, Aug. 23, 2017

Mnuchin may be the greatest sycophant in Cabinet history.
—Lawrence H. Summers, former Treasury secretary, Twitter, Sept. 24, 2017

Democrats on the House Financial Services Committee pressed Treasury Secretary Steven Mnuchin…to turn over records detailing any financial ties between President Donald Trump, his family and associates and Russian Interest. Mnuchin is "in the unique position of being able to assist Congress in assessing the extent of the Administration's financial entanglements with Russia."
—Associated Press, Dec. 8, 2017

Coal doesn't even make that much sense anymore as a feedstock.
—Gary Cohn, aboard Air Force One, May 26, 2017

Coal will be competitive again and the US needs to be ready.—Gary Cohn, CNBC, June 2, 2017

If we allow a family to keep another thousand dollars of their income, what does that mean? They can renovate their kitchen, they can buy a new car, they can take their family on vacation, they can increase their lifestyle.
—Gary Cohn, news conference, Sept. 28, 2017

Kudlow is a prolific cable news commentator who has a stellar reputation for being wrong—a lot. Like, *a lot a lot...* He has no formal education in economics… No matter the economic problem, it can be solved,
Kudlow promises, by cutting taxes for the wealthy and corporations.
 —Justin Miller, prospect.com, Dec. 21, 2016

Choosing to ignore the haywire,
In Patton, Trump found lots of fire:
For advice, his passing fancy
For some martial necromancy
When they will do what he requires.

Security Advisor **Flynn**
So quickly became a has-been;
Buried Russia conversations.
Then, with legal trepidation,
He became Mueller firing pin.

General McMaster took Flynn's place
With Ph.D as a showcase.
Against scrapping Iran accord;
Brought lots of wails from Bannon horde.
Moderates hoped for breathing space.

Mattis hailed Silicon Valley
As great military ally.
Learned about Syria quitting
By the @real DonaldTrump Twitting,
We waited for bad finale.

Trump went for the "Mad Dog" tag;
We hoped for "warrior monk" flag.
With generals getting the boot,
We now have worries more acute:
John Bolton with his body bags.

For immigrants, "extreme vetting";
With cronies, just perks place-setting.
Camaraderie does win out
Over any expertise clout.
Appointments help favor-getting.

Manage/Budget: **Mick Mulvaney**,
Tea-Partier news a-flamey.
Long wish-list for budget slashing:
Send social safety net crashing.
Mission worse than cockamamie.

General Flynn…What a good guy—Donald J. Trump, speech at CIA headquarters, twenty-four hours after inauguration. Flynn…one of Trump's most vocal campaign supporters …was already under FBI investigation…He had survived thirty-three years in the Army, but only twenty-four days in the White House—Greg Miller, *The Apprentice* (2018)

Trump proclaimed Retired Marine General Mattis "the closest thing we have to Gen. George Patton."
—Arthur Allen, *Politico*, Dec. 26, 2016

General McMaster, a war hero and a true soldier-scholar… is essentially a foreign-policy realist, though one with faith in the capacity of military action to effectuate security and stability…
—Jonathan Stevenson, *New York Times*, March 23, 2018

Mattis… hopes the tech industry will help the Pentagon catch up.—Tom Simonite, *Wired,* Aug. 11, 2017

Because you have the right to have a Secretary of Defense whose views are better aligned with yours on these and other subjects, I believe it is right for me to step down from my positions.—Defense Secretary James Mattis, letter to Donald Trump, Dec. 21, 2018

Mr. Mattis was the last of Mr. Trump's old-guard national security team—leaving policy in the hands of Mike Pompeo, the president's second secretary of state, and John R. Bolton, the third White House national security adviser.
—Helene Cooper, *New York Times*, Dec. 21, 2018

Bolton's ascendance increases the risk of not one but two wars—with North Korea and Iran. McMaster was no dove. But Bolton falls into an entirely different category of dangerous uber-hawk.
— Helene Cooper, *New York Times*, March 23, 2018

Loon of the Month John Bolton.
—Lucian K. Truscott IV, Salon, Dec. 22, 2018

Besides a Climate Change blockade,
He offers Meals-on-Wheels tirade.
Let 'em eat cake!
Or T-bone steak,
But cut off the government aid.

Then Mulvaney drew the short straw
With the "Acting Staff Chief" buzz saw.
Seeing danger on staff kebab,
Lots of bigwigs refused the job;
Mulvaney brings zealot chutzpah.

At commerce, we get **Wilbur Ross**,
Who helped casino albatross.
He thought job was money tilling;
In fact, science data drilling,
Where this blackguard is total loss.

Just for the fun of some "howdies,"
Went with Trump to see the Saudis,
No hint of protest, he hooted,
Note: Rebels get executed.
A bagman whose facts are cloudy.

Missile strike as entertainment;
Ross needs more mental containment.
Ross owns many works by Magritte:
Let's see Sago Mine balance sheet.
Where he should face an arraignment.

Labor's **Acosta** second choice,
But it's not reason to rejoice.
There's connection with vote caging
And suspect actions engaging.
No hope labor will get a voice.

Dr. Tom Price in loony pact;
His replacement is also fracked.
Azar: in big pharma pocket,
Raising prices on his docket.
Trump goal: Get health care whacked.

Apparently, not even the fundamentals of basic economic theory are safe form Mulvaney's zeal to aggrandize the wealthy at the expense of the poor.
—Taylor Lincoln, research director, Public Citizen, Congress Watch division, May 25, 2017

Mulvaney is a massive outlaw.—Ralph Nader, Democracy Now! Dec. 17, 2018

For the record, there were MANY people who wanted to be the White House Chief of Staff.—@realDonaldTrump, Twitter, Dec. 13, 2018

Wilbur Ross holds a stake in an offshore shipping company that is partnered with the son-in-law of Russian president Vladimir Putin.—Jon Swaine & Luke Harding, *The Guardian*, Nov. 5, 2017

When Ross sat…in front of the Commerce committee…there were few questions on his steel or textile conglomerates. The senators were chummy, tranquil, and distracted…the ranking Democrat commended Ross's wife for not letting her eyes wander during the proceedings.—Max Abelson, Bloomberg Businessweek, Jan. 26, 2017

Ross spent the majority of his first year in office as a business partner to the Chinese government, while he negotiated US-China trade relations.—Dan Alexander, Forbes, Aug. 7, 2018

Wilbur Ross seemed to have (to a comical degree) no clue that his new job was less about overseeing the nation's business than managing its scientific and census data.
—Jeremy Olshan, "Michael Lewis Takes on Trump and Weather in New Audiobook," Marketwatch, Aug. 1, 2018

During Azar's decade at Lilly, the company tripled the price of its insulin and was fined for colluding to keep its prices high in Mexico… "The last thing we need is to put a pharmaceutical executive in charge of the Department of Health and Human Services," said Sen. Bernie Sanders.
—Dina Fine Maron, *Scientific American*, Nov. 28, 2017

First, Trump wants Ayn Rand with M.D,
Now it's big pharma golden key.
This health pick is so so perverse,
Should travel to work in a hearse
Lined with full death's head gallery.

Working class gets austerity:
Warfare vendors reap great bounty,
Pentagon is insatiable,
Health benefits erasable.
Let's bring on the vigilantes.

Ryan Zinke: one more place kick:
Hunters and drillers get their pick.
Ever looking for profit nodes,
Shrink national monument codes,
And offer more White House gold brick.

Had eye on Alaska's North Slope;
Denning polar bears have no hope.
 "Technically recoverable oil,"
With no thought of what greed spoils,
Odious Big Money myope.

For neighbor, a deal of $300 million:
Puerto Rico fix cotillion.
$462 per hour for supervisor—
Quite a nifty money geyser.
Skill nil okay inTrump postillion.

Lots of moolah to be accrued
Bankroll $80 a day for food.
$332 budget for accommodation;
IRS allows small ration.
This should cause some disquietude.

At Ag there's **Gov. Sonny Perdue**—
Whoo-de-hee-dee-de-dee-hoo-hoo!
During drought he didn't complain,
But on state steps he prayed for rain.
Ignoring Climate Change boo-hoo.

Mr. Zinke arrived for his first day on horseback [horse named Tonto]…installed the arcade game Big Buck Hunter in the cafeteria…The Interior Department… is eliminating or preparing to reverse more than 150 Obama regulations, including those curtailing coal mining and hydraulic fracturing…It has reopened Alaska's Cook Inlet for business, made 76 million acres in the Gulf of Mexico available for offshore oil-and-gas exploration, and turbocharged pipeline permitting.—Kimberley A. Strassel, *Wall Street Journal*, Sept. 30,2017

[T]he only question, from the redwood forests to the Gulf Stream water, is how fast…resources can be auctioned off.
—Elizabeth Kolbert, *The New Yorker*, Jan 22, 2018

The President Stole Your Land…the largest elimination of protected land in American history.
—Patagonia homepage

Whitefish Energy, founded in 2015, signed a $300 million contract with Puerto Rico Electric Power Authority.
—Matthew Soza, Salon.com, Oct. 24, 2017

Whitefish Energy had only two full-time employees when the hurricane hit. But what it lacks in experience it makes up for in ties to the Trump administration.
—Bess Levin, *Vanity Fair* Hive, Oct. 24, 2017

Mr. Zinke is the latest Trump official to exit an administration beset by questions of ethical conflict…Rather than an end to Mr. Zinke's pro-fossil fuel policies, the resignation quite likely signals a passing of the playbook. Mr. Zinke's deputy, David Bernhardt, a former oil lobbyist…—Julie Turkewitz & Coral Davenport, *New York Times*, Dec. 15, 2018

Sonny's not of that chicken clan,
But he does have a school lunch plan.
Wants to make school eats great again—
Sugar, spice, salt and fat built in.
He's the frosted gingerbread man.

Dancing with Stars guy **Rick Perry**:
At Energy, he's quite scary.
Safeguarding nuclear weapons,
When he needs a mental trepan.
Hope for great brainwave Hail Mary.

What was in Rick's cha-cha profile
To task him nuclear stockpile?
Last expert: physics Ph.D.
Now it's a cerebral peewee.
In a quite dangerous turnstile.

Carson: Housing Development,
With plan of odd envelopment.
Calls Fair Housing "social engineering."
Instead, offer comfort shearing,
Do not give poor embellishment.

Says too much aid means dependence,
And poor won't work for ascendance.
Don't make housing for poor cozy;
Must work harder for world rosy.
Religious faith brings transcendence.

But out of the government pot
Ben found golden egg for his spot.
Ben Carson is in no cold sweat
For $31,000 office dining room set.
Blest precepts are just so much rot.

Vice-Prez vote brought billionaire seat
And push for Christian choice complete.
DeVos in charge of school districts.
Where she has thousands of critics
Who detail her hubris replete.

Agriculture Secretary Sonny Perdue announced that school meals would no longer have to meet some requirements connected with Mrs. Obama's initiative to combat childhood obesity by overhauling the nation's school menus.
—Erica I. Green & Julie Hirschfeld Davis, *New York Times*, May 1, 2017

Fossil fuels can help prevent sexual assault, Energy Secretary Rick Perry said Thursday…Perry also said that he does not believe that humans are the main drivers of climate change, telling the moderators Jim VandHei and "Meet the Press" host Chuck Todd, "I still think the science is out."
—Dartunorro Clark, NBC News, Nov. 2, 2017

It remains a liberal wet dream that a GOP-controlled Congress would impeach Trump, or that members of his Cabinet would invoke the 25th Amendment to yank him out of the White House (The notion of Ben Carson standing in judgment on anyone's mental health may be clinically insane in its own right.)
—Frank Rich, *New York*, Jan. 10, 2018

In his first public statement since Donald Trump chose him to be the Secretary of Housing and Urban Development, Ben Carson said on Monday that the Bible "makes absolutely no mention of housing or urban development."
—Andy Borowitz, *The New Yorker*, Dec. 5, 2016

HUD ordered a $31,000 dining-room set for Ben Carson's office—at the same time the department was planning to cut billions in public assistance for the poor.
—Daily Intelligence, March 3, 2018

Betsy DeVos, in charge of education issues, seems capable of losing at tic-tac-toe.
—Matt Taibbi, *Rolling Stone*, Aug. 27, 2017

Public policy banditry
Is found all in the family.
Brother, Blackwater Erik Prince,
Counsels Trump on martial evince,
In all ways, two calamities.

On public ed proficiency,
DeVos shows gross deficiency.
She cares about school armament—
For all grizzly bear bombardment
And wrongTitle IX fixity.

Head of public education
She who worked hard at predation.
Betsy DeVos has the money
To bring in the strived-for honey:
Public school privatization.

Pompeo headed CIA,
Tea Party; lifetime NRA.
Gave an award to Saudi prince,
And it was no flowering quince.
A plié in Trump Saudi ballet.

He was the Congressman from Koch,
Hospitable to their thick yoke.
Fan of corporate piracy;
Credits no right to privacy.
Fear of Muslims he does convoke.

Griped agency not tough enough,
Promised more vigor and rough stuff.
"Crush 'em" was his nifty motto.
Issued with shouting staccato,
He offered lots of suchlike chuff.

And now we can really grimace:
At State, Pompeo Maximus.
Bring on more torture and more war—
This guy is a carnivore,
Multiplying worldwide menace.

The United Arab Emirates arranged a secret meeting in January between Blackwater founder Erik Prince and a Russian close to President Vladimir Putin as part of an apparent effort to establish a back-channel line of communication between Moscow and President-elect Donald Trump.
—Ada Entous, Greg Miller, Kevin Sieff, & Karen DeYoung, *Washington Post*, April 3, 2017

Guns might belong in schools due to the threat posed by grizzly bears. Betsy DeVos, Donald Trump's nominee to head the Department of Education, told senators on Tuesday.
—Sabrina Siddiqui, *The Guardian*, Jan. 18, 2017

Betsy DeVos and her relatives have given at least $20.2 million to Republican candidates, party committees, PACs and super PACs since 1989.
—Center for Responsive Politics, Dec. 1, 2016

We expect to foster a conservative governing philosophy consisting of limited government and respect for traditional American values.—Betsy DeVos, *Roll Call*, Sept. 6, 1997

While in Congress, Mr. Pompeo argued for domestic surveillance on a wide scale, insisted that waterboarding was not torture and dismissed a hunger strike by detainees at Guantanamo Bay as a 'political stunt."—Matthew Rosenberg, *New York Times,* Aug. 7, 2017

Mike Pompeo, nominee for Director of the CIA, is a 3 out of 5 on the Swamp-O-meter. He's been a politician for 6 years, has been bankrolled by and is beholden to the Kochs, and has accused American Muslims of being complicit in terrorist attacks. Can you spell swamp?
—*Washington Monthly*, Dec. 14, 2016

Why bother with global pie charts?
Climate info comes from Breibart.
Picking up mantras from Twitter,
Trump chose climate change hard hitter
Who uses Bible for restart.

At Environment, **Scott Pruitt**,
The governor who did sue it,
Using corporate money tools
In attempts to stop climate rules,
Now he sits in screw-it cockpit.

Times Pulitzer for exposure;
But Senate ignored disclosures.
With a bounder so scurrilous,
Climate boneheads are worriless,
Applauding their Trump enclosure.

Pruitt's views fit superbly in
With The Donald's old climate spin:
You know, light bulbs can cause cancer,
Global Warming is dung answer
To China-created news din.

At transportation, **Elaine Chao**
Brings lots of insider know-how.
She did have the same job before,
And sees the political score.
She knows with whom she can pow-wow.

Nepotism is way of life:
Mitch can just giggle with his wife.
For Chao, everything is rosy.
And if anyone gets nosy,
She just brings out the butter knife.

Scientist for Ag lacked knowledge;
Came with lots of race slur haulage.
Sam Clovis: Rural whisperer:
And a climate change silencer.
Crashed in Papadopoulos pillage.

This very expensive GLOBAL WARMING bullshit has got to stop. Our planet is freezing, record low temps, and our GW scientists are stuck in ice.
—@realDonaldTrump, Twitter, Jan. 1, 2014

Pruitt used the Bible to explain major changes in the composition of the agency's independent advisory committees…What the "Joshua Principle" means for the EPA is that scientists who receive agency grants for their research are now barred from serving on any of its independent advisory boards. This opens the door to more industry and political representation.
—Rebecca Leber, *Mother Jones,* Oct. 31, 2017

Remember new 'environmentally friendly' lightbulbs can cause cancer.
—@realDonaldTrump, Twitter, Oct. 17, 2012

The concept of global warming was created by and for the Chinese in order to make U.S. manufacturing non-competitive.
—@realDonaldTrump, Twitter, Nov. 6, 2012

Transportation Secretary Elaine Chao said she supports both her husband, Senate Majority Leader Mitch McConnell, and President Trump amid the commander in chief's ongoing fight with the senator. "I stand by my man—both of them" Chao told reporters.
—Melanie Zanona, *The Hill*, Aug. 25, 2017

Sam Clovis, Mr. Trump's nomination to be the Agriculture Department's chief scientist, is not a scientist. He's a former talk-radio host and incendiary blogger who has labeled climate research "junk science."
—Editorial Board, *New York Times*, Sept. 9, 2017

Nickki Haley at UN spot
Seemed to some an apt Trump hook shot,
Echoing there his ridicule
For orthodox policy tools.
But follow-up shows more brain rot.

Stephen Miller, young advisor,
Penned "American carnage" geyser.
Spoke of Trump's substantial powers
"Will not be questioned"— Do cower—
Confusing Trump with the Kaiser.

Bannon put Miller on this ledge:
Vicious anti-immigrant sledge.
At the center of gravity
For messages depravity,
He's a total Trump slime-ball wedge.

Shulkin at Veteran Affairs
Seemed to have a true golden chair.
Congress sounded loud the bugle!
Only choice with full approval.
Then trouble came with airline fares.

Asked if he'd ever lied on job,
Sean Spicer offered a huge lob.
Said he'd not "knowingly" done so.
News folk did dance the fandango,
While he waggled a total glob.

Hicks led communications squad,
Once Scarmucci, did talk unshod,
Aft Spicer, who spurred McCarthy's
SNL saga quite smarty,
Aft Dubke who left: no applaud.

Hicks, once model for Ralph Lauren,
Showcased Ivanka's wares end run.
Long rising star in Trump orbit
Sometimes it's hard to absorb it:
White House stars emerge from warren.

[Heather Nauert, former anchor on Fox News and friend of Ivanka and Jared], the woman who would soon become President Trump's pick to represent the United States at the United Nations cited the D-Day landings...to showcase the strength of German-American relations.
—Isaac Stanley-Becker, *Washington Post*, Dec. 7, 2018

Heather Nauert Says Visit to "It's a Small World" Ride Qualifies Her For U.N. Job—Andy Borowitz, *The New Yorker*, Dec. 7, 2018

Fox News Intern Fetching Coffee Tells Herself This Will All Pay Off When She's Trump's Secretary Of State One Day
—The Onion, Dec. 7, 2018

The childhood rabbi to Stephen Miller... a key architect of [Trump's] "zero-tolerance" immigration policies, criticized his former charge as a purveyor of "negativity, violence, malice and brutality" who had learned nothing from his Jewish spiritual education.
—Andrew Gumbel, *The Guardian*, Sept. 10, 2018

Conservative radio host Rush Limbaugh...said that although Bannon is out, the White House will be okay because policy advisor Stephen Miller is still on staff
"and Stephen Miller is a gem."
—Amber Athey, The Daily Caller, Aug. 28, 2017

Inside the White House, Miller has emerged as a staunch ideologue and an immigration hawk championing an agenda of right-wing nationalism.
—McKay Coppins, *The Atlantic*, May 28, 2018

After moving to New York [Hicks] worked for an advertising agency that handled the Ivanka Trump brand. From there she was brought into the Trump organization to work on Miss Trump's fashion line.
—Nick Allen, *The Telegraph*, Sept. 13, 2017

Eric's wed planner oversees
Housing/Development money.
Let's not offer discouragements:
Also did run golf tournaments.
And **Patton** slings verbal debris.

Schiller: From watch dog to Operations;
Dan Scavino has new station:
Special mini-me assistant.
In old pals Trump is consistent.
Never mind needs of the nation.

Omarosa, was also there.
Offering her own distinct blare.
She yelled, while barnstorming on stump,
All should "bow down to Donald Trump."
Quite a blitz of PR nightmare.

Then she just decided to scoot—
Or Chief Kelly gave her the boot.
As often, someone was lying.
But we don't hear any crying.
She was known for chaos acute.

From World Wrestling Entertainment
Came yet another guild claimant:
McMahon, founding CEO,
A fixture with bushels of dough,
Donned Small Business Admin raiment.

Long history with wrestling world,
Put Trump's WrestleMania twirl
Into WWE Hall of Fame.
No other prez can make this claim.
Shows what occurs in hype-filled swirl.

Galaviz, Casino front gate,
To job at Department of State.
Harleth, hotel director rooms,
To White House Chief Usher job zooms,
Leaving tradition buffs irate.

Lynne Patton, a former event planner for Eric Trump, was appointed… to oversee all federal housing in New York and New Jersey… Patton said her experience as "gatekeeper to one of the most powerful families in the world" qualified her for the position. Now, Patton is spending her time lobbing ugly insults at journalists on Twitter.
—Judd Legum, ThinkProgress, Jan. 24, 2018

Keith Schiller…former bodyguard [and] one of the president's closest confidants outside his family…has also acted as Trump's hatchet man…told James Comey that the president has decided to fire him as FBI director.
—Shannon Pettypiece and Jennifer Jacobs. Bloomberg, Sept. 5, 2017

Scavino was among the staffers Trump invited to join him at the Vatican to meet the pope.
—Eliana Johnson, *Politico*, June 10, 2017

[In 9 weeks on "The Apprentice," Omarosa Manigault] was portrayed as a cut-throat contestant…served as Trump campaign's director of African-American outreach and will now serve as White House political aide.
—CNBC, Jan. 3, 2017

Trump's appearance on "Monday Night Raw" and "WrestleMania" were scripted… but his professional wrestling character was remarkably in keeping with his actual persona…He was brash, belittling and comfortably stirring up crowds of rowdy supporters.
—Paul Farhi, *Washington Post*, Dec. 26, 2015

Linda McMahon donated $6 million to the super PAC, Rebuilding America Now, formed in the summer of 2016 when Mr. Trump's presidential campaign was short of cash.—Sharon LaFraniere, Maggie Haberman & Adam Goldman, *New York Times*, Dec. 18, 2018

[Jonathan Galaviz's casino consulting firm] consults for at least two Russian state entities, according to its website—proudly announced that Galaviz would be back after his stint at State. Galaviz himself consulted for a Russian government corporation on casino gambling.
—Betsy Woodruff, Daily Beast, July 19, 2017

Times past, Usher term did not end
With new person coming to tend.
J.P. West served four presidents.
And others had long residence.
Trump has no use for such a trend.

FBI **James Comey** stood tall.
Maybe it's reason for his fall.
Taller than Trump by five inches,
Maybe too big for his britches.
Shrinkage seemed like part of the brawl.

Taking the cloak of royalty,
Trump insisted on loyalty.
Comey stood for independence,
Jarring Yuge with Trump's resplendence.
In work as well as toiletry.

Then the ever-loaded cannon,
The alternate prez **Steve Bannon**.
Man Behind Curtain with straight flush,
In catbird seat, then underbrush,
Fancied himself quite a shaman.

Worked "enemies of Trump" trolling:
Ryan and Cohen sink-holing.
The far-right conniving Brahmin,
Publicly gone but no hush man.
He's still politics patrolling.

Keep a close eye on news Breitbart,
With its pulpit for Bannon darts.
No one is more media slick,
Ever there with hard right dipstick.
On Democrats, he has jump-start.

Just remember *Schadenfreude*.
What he'll do when really annoyed.
Bannon sees self as kingmaker,
Working deals on Trump's Yuge acre.
Won't give a fig for what's destroyed.

Timothy Harleth will serve as White House chief usher, leaving his position at the Trump International Hotel.
—Politico, June 23, 2016

On "60 Minutes" former White House chief strategist Steve Bannon said he believes Trump's firing of James Comey to be the biggest mistake in "modern political history."—Miranda Green & Jeremy Diamond, CNN, Sept. 11, 2017

This Republican Congress has proven incapable of fulfilling the Founders' design that "Ambition must ... counteract ambition." All who believe in this country's values must vote for Democrats this fall. Policy differences don't matter right now. History has its eyes on us.—James Comey, Twitter, July 17, 2018

Steve Bannon is the love child of Darth Vader and Leni Riefenstahl.
—Joy Behar, *The Great Gasbag: An A-to-Z Study Guide to Surviving Trump World* (2017)

Bannon: is very smart and very energetic; what he lacks is even a trace of *moral* intelligence.
—Martin Amis, *Esquire,* Nov. 2017

Jerry Falwell, Jr., the president of Liberty University and one of the most influential leaders in the evangelical Christian community nationwide, is calling for evangelicals everywhere to stand with Stephen K. Bannon against the "Fake Republicans."
—Matthew Lyon, Breitbart News, Oct. 25, 2017

"The longer they talk about identity politics, I got 'em." he said. "I want them to talk about racism every day. If the left is focused on race and identity, and we go with economic nationalism, we can crush the Democrats."
—Steve Bannon to Robert Kuttner, *The American Prospect*, Aug. 26, 2017

The President of the United States is a great man. You know I support him day in and day out.
—Steve Bannon, Breitbart News Tonight, Jan. 3, 2018

Bannon spilled the beans on Junior
For his behavior peculiar.
Now former pals are on the outs
Trump issues anti-Bannon shouts.
All of interest to Mueller.

Mercers paid for seats at table;
Call Robert co-prez de-stable.
Yikes! Cambridge Analytica,
Voter psycho perfectica.
They do the Alt-Right enable.

Dark foundations: sign of the times,
Supplying the White House job prime—
With presence of great annoyers:
Even Trump's lawyers have lawyers,
Working through the slime.

When **Conway** was steaming for Cruz,
She issued Trump a heavy bruise.
Employing some rhetoric vile.
But now The Donald gets her smile.
Just part of politico ooze.

Kellanne Conway, Mercer pick,
Riding in on Bannon's broomstick,
Basic verbiage she did redact,
Bringing us "alternative facts."
Counselor to the prez, she's slick.

Doubling as personal shopper,
With some Ivanka name droppers.
Ivanka, the supreme brander,
Does offer swelled head and pander:
Wholly a Donald sharecropper.

Labeling impresario,
This woman knows how the dough flows.
Taking chairs in meddlesome spots
And hosting dinners for big shots
To sway how lawmaking wind blows.

I have always loved investigations. I love everything about investigations. One of the most challenging times I've had as a lawyer has been doing homicides in DC. I love the forensics. I love the fingerprints and the bullet casings and all the rest that comes along with doing that kind of work."—Robert Mueller to Cullen Couch, *UVA Lawyer*, Fall 2002

[Robert Mercer] put ten million dollars into Breitbart News…[and] some five million dollars in Cambridge Analytica, a firm that mines online data to reach and influence potential voters. The company has said that
it uses secret psychological methods to pinpoint which messages are the most persuasive to individual online viewers… William Kristol, the editor of *The Weekly Standard* and an adamant Trump opponent, warned,
"It's the mergers of the Trump campaign with the
Kooky right."
—Jane Mayer, *The New Yorker*, March 27, 2017

President Donald Trump's counselor Kellyanne Conway said White House press secretary Sean Spicer used "alternative facts" when he falsely called the crowds at Trump's swearing-in ceremony "the largest audience to ever witness an inauguration.
—Mahita Gajanan, *Time*, Jan. 22, 2017

Since [Trump] has no fixed ideology, the White House cannot screen for ideas, so it seeks a more personal form of devoted attendants, refers reverently to the "October 8th coalition," the campaign stalwarts who remained at Trump's side while the world listened to a recording of him boasting about grabbing women by the genitals.
—Evan Osnos, *The New Yorker, May 21, 2018*

First daughter Ivanka Trump is hosting GOP lawmakers for dinner to garner support for her latest political push.
—Avery Anapol, *The Hill*, Oct. 10, 2017

Ivanka's Instagram is a key part of her Fascist Barbie brand.—Gaby Del Valle, The Outline, Jan. 24, 2018

Jared, in tenets pliable,
Looking more and more friable.
Some emphasize he's quite savvy;
There's evidence he's just grabby,
Greedy drone undeniable.

The Jarvankas star in playbill.
Ever selling the Trump Fable.
As they're claiming benefaction,
They offer ready distraction
On the Trump spinning turntable.

Call them just what they are: Grifters.
Lush and highfalutin' sifters
With opportunity and fame,
And policy ploys worse than lame:
These two Trump silver-tongued twisters.

We saw them here,
We saw them there:
The Kushners go whereso they want—
When the need suits, with their *e'nfants*.
We see and hear them everywhere.

Ivanka has expressed craving
From Oval Office to be waving.
Ivanka as first prez female?
We won't say "Molotov cocktail,"
But stop! It's a notion depraving.

Priebus: Short stay as Chief of Staff.
Controlling egress caused great chaff.
Gen. John Kelly was replacement:
Military-style emplacement
For regulating House riffraff.

Ruling face-time with president,
Gauging office entry assent.
Couldn't change TrumpTV habits,
Jam-packed with the Alt Facts maggots.
Nor decrease the free-fall events.

Jared Kushner, President Trump's son-in-law and senior advisor, was forwarded a document about a "Russian backdoor overture" that Mr. Kushner failed to hand over to the panel's investigators…Nor did he hand over other communications with a Russian-born businessman that were forwarded him…The Senate panel said that Mr. Kushner has also not produced records that investigators believe exist.—Michael S. Schmidt, *New York Times*, Nov. 16, 2017

The railhead of all bad decisions is the same railhead. Javanka.—Steve Bannon to Gabriel Sherman, *Vanity Fair*, Dec. 21, 2017

In April, when President Xi Jinping was visiting Trump at his Mar-a-Lago estate, Trump's granddaughter sang a Chinese folksong the Chinese president's wife had once performed on Chinese television. "We wanted to make you feel at home," Ivanka told Xi. In July while *New York Times* reporter was interviewing Trump, in pops Ivanka with Arabella.
Trump: She speaks fluent Chinese. ..Say, like, 'love you, Grandpa.'
Arabella: Wo ai ni, Grandpa.
Peter Baker, *New York Times*: That's great.
—Clio Chang, *The New Republic*, July 24, 2017

The president on occasion has called White House aides to the private residence in the evening, where he makes assignments and asks them not to tell Mr. Kelly about the plans.
—Michael C. Bender, *Wall Street Journal*, Dec. 3, 2017

Kelly told the White House press corps how disgusted he was that an "empty barrel" like [Congresswoman] Wilson could hog the spotlight at such a somber occasion. Except, it wasn't true.
—Ledyard King, *USA Today*, Oct. 21, 2017

While some officials had predicted Mr. Kelly would be a calming chief of staff for an impulsive president, recent days have made clear that his is more aligned with President Trump than anticipated.
—Peter Baker, *New York Times*, Oct. 26, 2017

Kelly caught in enormous lies
In eagerness to demonize
A loud voice of criticism.
One more goose step toward fascism:
White House fright does metastasize.

As to refugee admission,
Kelly argued for abscission,
Outdoing even Trump's blowgun
Sounding like saurischian:
Let in between zero and one.

Wrap-up

Trump swears, "I'll give you everything."
From highland fling to shiny bling,
The Art of the Deal phantasy:
"I play to people's fantasies."
Someone, please please, check the O-ring.

Yes, "We will have so much winning
That you may get bored with winning...
Believe me." Me. Me Me Me Me.
Trump offers his Tweedle-de-dee.
Are we spooked yet? Or just spinning.

Richest admin in history
Looks like perfect pitch piggery.
Sky's the limit when hiring friends
Who can pay off in dividends,
Pure capitalist sophistry.

Money ethos residency
Makes for-profit presidency.
Everyone in his cabinet
Prospers in tax plan flatulent.
Greed Squad without hesitancy.

Golf courses eat chlorpyrifos,
Promoters are politicos.
So The Donald appoints Pruitt
Someone quite trusty to do it:
We got a golf frontier hero.

Kelly didn't suddenly become a racist dickbag when the leaves turned," Samantha Bee noted. "Before he was chief of staff… Kelly was the guy in charge of two of Trump's most racist policies: banning Muslims and deporting Mexicans.
—Elias Leight, *Rolling Stone*, Nov. 2, 2018

In the countries they come from, fourth,- fifth-, sixth-grade educations are kind of the norm…They don't speak English. They don't integrate well. They don't have skills. They're not bad people. They're coming here for a reason. And I sympathize with the reason. But the laws are the laws.
—John Kelly, NPR, May 11, 2018

General John Kelly has taken the helm at the Trump White House. This must be understood as a declaration of all-out war against immigrant families.
—People's Congress of Resistance, Aug. 2, 2017

The retired Marine general was brought in to tame the president, but in the end Trump boxed him in.
—Eliana Johnson, *Politico*, July 29, 2018

[W]ith the exception of the late great Abraham Lincoln, I can be more presidential than any president that's ever held this office. That I can tell you. It's real easy.
—Donald Trump, Youngstown, Ohio, Aug. 26, 2017

"He's an idiot. It's pointless to try to convince him of anything. He's gone off the rails. We're in Crazytown. I don't even know why any of us are here. This is the worst job I've ever had." —John Kelly on President Trump in Bob Woodward, *Fear: Trump in the White* House (2018)

The Clean Water Rule enables the government to prevent pollution in fresh water wetlands and streams, which are sources of drinking water for about 117 million Americans… In practice, it means that facilities that house pollutants and are located near water sources are subject to stricter requirements to prevent those waters from being contaminated.
—Honorable David N. Cicilline and Rick Claypool, Public Citizen, Oct. 11, 2017

Twelve Trump golf courses in U.S.
That Clean Water Rule does oppress.
Trump calls the law just horrible
And prefers it ignorable;
Just call this golf magnate's noblesse.

So Pruitt rejected the ban
Showing that a canner can can.
He named "reliable data";
Specialists say bogus strata.
First he's the best man, then drip pan.

It's the "Let them eat cake" dictum,
Capitalist benediction.
We get the Trump imprimatur:
"Just let them drink dirty water."
No Congress to contradict him.

Forsake all food label alerts
That challenge corporate pay dirt.
Trump's rotund oratorio:
Larder with Cokes and Oreos.
And don't try to sugar avert.

Opposed breast milk resolution
In aid of big biz ablution.
Threatened disagreeing nations
Who spoke against exploitation.
Babies suffer Trump pollution.

And then something hugely scary:
Electric grid head Rick Perry:
Yell chief at Texas A & M,
Endangering us with mayhem
Like amoebic dysentery.

Former guy with nuclear key
Was head of physics, MIT,
With top technologies nexus.
Rick was "Top Cowboy of Texas."
Just go float your rubber duckie.

Eagle Sign and Design, a company with offices in New Albany, Indiana, and Louisville, Kentucky, said it had received an order to manufacture dozens of round, 12-inch replicas of the presidential seal to be placed next to the tee boxes at Trump golf course holes…An order form for the tee markers…says the customer was "Trump International" … A law governs the manufacture or use of the seal, its likeness, "or any facsimile thereof" for anything other than official U.S. government business.
—Katherine Sullivan, *ProPublica*, March 5, 2018

Chalk one up for the swamp. The permanent progressive state finally ran Scott Pruitt out of the Environmental Protection Agency.
—Editorial, *Wall Street Journal*, July 5, 2018

Just when America had all but given up hope, Scott Pruitt's appalling reign as Environmental Protection Agency administrator is finally over.
—Editorial, *New York Times*, July 5, 2018

[T]here are only a few physical remnants of Pruitt's time at the EPA — namely a largely unused, $43,000 sound-proof phone booth…— Juliet Eilperin, Brady Dennis, Brady Dennis & Josh Dawsey, *Washington Post*, Dec. 28, 2018

Urged on by big food and soft-drink companies, the Trump administration is using the trade talks with Mexico and Canada to try to limit the ability of the pact's three members—including the United States—to warn consumers about the dangers of junk food.
—Azam Ahmed, Matt Richtel, & Andrew Jacobs, *New York Times*, March 20, 2018

What happened was tantamount to blackmail, with the U.S. holding the world hostage and trying to overturn nearly 50 years of consensus on the best way to protect infant and young child health.—Patti Rundall, policy director of the Baby Milk Action, *New York Times* Quotation of the Day, July 8, 2018

"[Perry' has no personal interest in understanding what we do and effecting change," a D.O.E. staffer told me in June. "He's never been briefed on a program—not a single one."
—Michael Lewis, *Vanity Fair*, Sept. 2017

Ulysses Grant launched Park System:
Now Trump brings earth cataclysm.
Huge rollback of land protection
Allows oil and gas extraction.
Mining, logging, profit schisms.

Zap ban on beast trophy import;
Big game hunters can still cavort.
Zinke and his advisory team
Of NRA and spoils regime
Call heads, hides, and horns grab a sport.

The Saudis pay Boeing big bucks,
Clearly, this is not for dump trucks.
Depicted as planes for defense,
While Yemen bombing is immense.
Response to this horror: "Aw, shucks."

Some words you can say when you want:
George Carlin named seven don't flaunt.
Trump staff has added forbiddens—
Words they banish to the midden.
"Evidenced-based" is truly gaunt.

Trump blasts about countries shithole;
With no thought of status or soul.
Who in Congress can stop this yup
And get him clinical work-up?
Needed: White House disease control.

Netanyahu loves his great wall
And this notion does Trump enthrall.
The two are in comfy accord
In defining marauding hordes.
Now who's the worse Neanderthal?

Defended by Fox News host-man,
On speaking for forgotten clan.
"This's how Trump relates to peoples"—
Showing he's a racist creeple
With a hubris watering can.

A new US advisory board created to help rewrite federal rules for importing the heads and hides of African elephants, lions and rhinos is stacked with trophy hunters …Among Zinke's appointees is Steven Chancellor, a longtime Republican fundraiser… According to Safari Club member hunting records… Chancellor has logged nearly 500 kills—including at least 18 lions, 13 leopards, six elephants and two rhinos.
—Michael Biesecker, Jake Pearson, & Jeff Horwitz, Associated Press, March 25, 2018

Donald J. Trump State Park, Westchester County, NY. When Trump couldn't get town permits to develop 436 acres as golf course, he donated land to New York State, claiming $100 million tax write-off. It sits abandoned and in total disrepair.—AV News, Feb. 18, 2017

Policy analysts at the Centers for Disease Control and Prevention were told of the list of forbidden words: "vulnerable," "entitlement," "diversity," "transgender," "fetus," "evidence-based" and "science-based."
—Lena H. Sun & Juliet Eilperin, *Washington Post*, Dec. 15, 2017

This is how the forgotten men and women of America talk at the bar…This is who Trump is…and if he offends some people, fine.
—Jesse Watters, Fox News host, Jan 12, 2018

It belongs to the genius of a great leader to make even adversaries far removed from one another seem to belong to a single category…so that in the eyes of the masses of one's own supporters the struggle is directed against only one enemy. This strengthens their faith in their own right and enhances their bitterness against those who attack it.
—Adolf Hitler, *Mein Kampf* (1929, 20th edition 1999)

The FAKE NEWS media (failing @nytimes, @NBC News, @ABC, @CBS, @CNN) is not my enemy, it is the enemy of the American People!
—@realDonaldTrump, Twitter, Feb. 17, 2017

Fox News is no longer the propaganda arm of the Republican Party. The Republican Party is the legislative arm of Fox News.
—David Atkins, *Washington Monthly*, Dec. 22, 2018

Popular sophistry sharer,
Limbaugh applauds reign of error.
Agrees there's no climate change—
Along with other themes deranged.
Trump pal: Hatred standard-bearer.

Trump ignores team consultation.
Cause for exultation?
Or panic?
This is an issue gigantic:
Fear of prez ego inflation.

And here are a few more questions
About Trump moral ablation.
What about tax returns he skates?
Does conduct outdo Watergate?
Congress should feel indigestion.

Stormy: pro tem competition:
Publicity-seeking fission.
Yes, she submitted quite a case
That Trump found awkward to erase.
$130,000 bucks is good fruition.

Press that run Russia documents About the White House occupant Get "Enemy of People" brand.
Next will come the warning armbands
From our leader incontinent.

Hopes for national calm shatter When White House is press batterer. How can leader contribute calm
At same time he is tossing bombs? We just wait for the next splatter.

He of politico thin skin
Launches hate-filled Twitter whirlwind.
With psyche acrimonious,
Finds SNL felonious,
Urging freedom of press depin.

You're a very special man, Rush, and you have people that love you. I'm one of them. What you do for this country, people have no idea how important your voice is. This is your favorite president, and I think you are fantastic.—Donald Trump calling in to congratulate Rush Limbaugh on the 30th anniversary of his radio show, Aug. 1, 2018

MSNBC: Putin kills journalists who don't agree with him. Donald Trump: At least he's a leader, unlike what we have in this country. I think our country does plenty of killing also.—MSNBC *Morning Joe*, Dec. 2015

Russia currently ranks 180 out of 199 countries for press freedom, behind Iraq, Sudan, and the Democratic Republic of Congo.—Linda Qiu, PunditFact, Jan 4, 2016

President Trump did not follow specific warnings from his national security advisers when he congratulated Russian President Vladimir Putin on his reelection—including a section in his briefing materials in all-capital letters stating "DO NOT CONGRATULATE."—Carol D. Leonnig, David Nakamura, & Josh Dawsey, *Washington Post*, Mar 21, 2018

"Shameful," "Treasonous," "Disgraceful"; Trump slammed from all sides for news conference with Putin.
—NBC news headline, July 16, 2018

With millions wondering if Vladimir Putin has damaging info about Trump, and suspecting they have a secret pact, the president does something almost unheard of in history. He meets alone with Putin for two hours. Then… the president shows so much deference at their press conference you would think he was meeting with the Pope.—Mike Allen, Axios, July 28, 2018

The Summit with Russia was a great success, except with the real enemy of the people, the Fake News Media.
 —@realDonaldTrump, Twitter, July 19, 2018

Each Jew is the sworn enemy of the Jewish people. If someone wears the Jewish star, he is an enemy of the people. Anyone who deals with him is the same as a Jew and must be treated accordingly.—Joseph Goebbels, Reich Minister of Propaganda, Nov. 16, 1941

For Trump, villains have to be found;
He wants enemies underground.
The Prez has got a lengthy list—
The Prez has got a lengthy list—
Of those he wants to kick around.

With Trump comfortably at the prow,
We get corporation kow-tow
With Evangelic infusion,
And vile immigrant exclusion,
Revoking our national vow.

This is a dilemma acute:
National values in dispute.
The Oval Office shouts horror.
Our answer: Statute restorer.
Stop this Constitution uproot.

Stop this regime of greed and Id,
Putting all our lives on the skid.
Stop mocking of moral accords,
Putting bigotry on TV scoreboards.
Remove Trump from the power grid.

Back to his Versailles he should go
 "No return" ticket in cargo.
Not one of the Trumps will be missed.
And not one of them will be missed
Their departure will leave us aglow.

No room, you tired, you poor,
Wretched refuse at teeming shore.
Huddled masses yearning to breathe free,
No room here for tempest-tossed: Flee!
Trump has deadlocked the golden door.

Unlike most perceived presidential adversaries, about whom Mr. Trump is rarely shy, Ms. Clifford [Stormy Daniels] has not been the subject of a single tweet.—Matt Flegenheimer, Rebecca R. Ruiz, & Katie Van Syckle, *New York Times*, March 24, 2018

A REAL scandal is the one sided coverage, hour by hour, of networks like NBC & Democrat spin machines like Saturday Night Live. It is all nothing less than unfair news coverage and Dem commercials. Should be tested in courts, can't be legal? Only defame & belittle! Collusion?
—@realDonaldTrump,Twitter, Dec. 16, 2018
[The President sent out 10 Twitter flames on this day.]

Trump's world view is tragic for so many reasons. First, he's just wrong on the basics. As the Republican pollster Frank Luntz tweeted, "43% of immigrants from 'shithole' African countries have a bachelor's degree or higher compared to 33% of the overall American population.
—Robin Wright, *The New Yorker*, Jan. 12, 2018

Why are we having all these people from s---hole countries come here?" the president said…About a dozen people, including both Republicans and Democrats, were in the room at the time …The president also suggested the United States should admit more people from countries like Norway instead.—Alex Pappas, Fox News, Jan. 11, 2018

We should have built a wall
—Native American T-shirt

While Trump preaches perversity,
The nation wants diversity.
In Trump hatred shrouded,
Lady's lamp is clouded.
We must stop this perfidy

Never forget the causation
Of our great station:
Life, liberty, and good chance
Are not happenstance:
Our land built on immigration.

My country 'tis of thee,
For sale: Purple mountains majesty.
Now sick land of Trumpetry.
Land where our fathers died,
Bring back our heritage pride,
Not billionaires beatified,
From sea to shining sea.

I don't want to get into a whole thing about history here…but the poem that you're referring to was added later (and) is not actually part of the original Statue of Liberty.—Stephen Miller, White House senior policy advisor and speechwriter, Aug. 3, 2017

Donald Trump drew more than typical stares when he took to the field at the college football national championship in Atlanta; he incurred the wrath and mockery of eagle-eyed TV viewers who noted that the current U.S. president didn't seem to know the words to the national anthem.—Joyce Chen, *Rolling Stone*, Jan. 9, 2018

Trump Demands Poem on Statue of Liberty Be Revised to Exclude Shithole Countries—Andy Borowitz, *The New Yorker*, Jan. 12, 2018

VI TRUMPED OUT: Rundown

Gramps Trump born in Bavaria,
But then he left the area.
When he decided to return,
His repatriation was spurned,
And Grandpa felt hysteria.

Son Fred wanted to keep up schmooze
With his clientele who were Jews,
So Trumps said Grandpa was a Swede.
In his bios, this antecede
The Donald did boldly infuse.

'73 Justice let Trump know
Suit over rental fandango.
"Antiblack bias": *Times* headline.
Donald, ever bottled in brine,
Burst forth with denials aglow.

For Trump, everything "arrangement"—
Not open building engagement.
With immigrant "Polish Brigade,"
Infamous for Bonwit degrade,
It was all about assuagement.

Trump had made promise to the Met
That Deco façade they would get.
Then came the typical fleeces,
Deco jackhammered in pieces.
The tale of Trump Tower asset.

All Beaux-Arts reliefs were destroyed,
And higher costs Trump did avoid.
Workers had to sue to get paid.
After years, settlement was made,
Keeping lots of lawyers employed.

From a letter written in 1905 by Frederich Trump, Donald Trump's grandfather, to Luitpold, prince regent of Bavaria. Trump had been ordered to leave Bavaria for failing to complete mandatory military service and to register his initial emigration to the United States twenty years earlier. Prince Luitpold rejected Trump's request for repatriation; the family later settled in New York.
"We were paralyzed with fright; our happy family life was tarnished…Why should we be deported? This is very, very hard for a family…"—*Harper's* March 2017

I suppose Old Man Trump knows
Just how much Racial Hate
He stirred up
In the bloodpot of human hearts
When he drawed That color line
Here at his Eighteen hundred family project
—Woody Guthrie, "Old Man Trump," ~1950

[Trump] had promised the [Bonwit-Teller] Limestone reliefs to the Metropolitan Museum of Art…But suddenly workmen jackhammered them to bits…The Trump organization replied that the two-ton parcels were "without artistic merit," that saving them would have delayed construction for months and cost $500,000.
—Charles Gray, *New York Times*, Oct. 3, 2014

[Undocumented Polish Workers'] treatment led to years of litigation over Mr. Trump's labor practices, and in 1998, despite frequent claims that he never settles lawsuits, Mr. Trump quietly reached an agreement to end a class-action suit over the Bonwit-Teller demolition in which he was a defendant. [The workers were paid as little as $4 an hour for their dangerous labor, less than half the union wage, if they got paid at all.]—Charles V. Bagli, *New York Times*, Nov. 37, 2017

Result secret for twenty years
So The Donald could avoid smears
That he ever settles lawsuits.
But workers did receive earned fruits,
So for the plaintiffs, give three cheers.

The judge ruled that Trump did cheat
But for art there's no balance sheet.
Breaking a promise about art
Gets cries only from bleeding hearts—
Just more poop on a Yuge deadbeat.

The Donald shrugged this mess off
Without disturbing his fine coif.
From his bottom-line perspective,
He met his money objective:
Non-stop feeding at profits trough.

Building height is part of the show.
Trump adds on ten stories or so.
His height and hands also a scam
Selling schemes for magna con man:
Inventing mojo for more dough.

To plan diversity's downfall,
Trump boasts, "I will build a great wall."
"This will make America great."
But such ugliness just deflates.
His instructions greatly appall.

Just evaluate each fine mess:
Iron Curtain and Berlin: yes.
Those who don't learn from history…
Of course, repeat the misery.
Will he bring back Pony Express?

Wall of China was great. Trump said,
Many miles stop alien tread.
"That wall, nobody does get through,
That I can tell you."
Thirteen thousand miles of blockhead.

[L]esson from that experience: good publicity is preferable to bad but from a bottom-line perspective, bad publicity is sometimes better than no publicity at all.
—Donald J. Trump, *Trump: The Art of the Deal* (1987)

"Donald Trump is the father of this," said Richard Wallgren, director of sales at the AOL building…" He'd say, 'This building has 75 stories.' Of course, when you counted, they were missing 10 stories because he gave the lobby 15 stories… and apartments would start on 16."
—Ralph Gardner, Jr., *New York Times*, May 8, 2003

I play to people's fantasies…People want to believe that something is the biggest and the greatest…I call it truthful hyperbole, It's an innocent form of exaggeration—and a very effective form of promotion.
—Donald J. Trump, *Trump: The Art of the Deal* (1987)

I will build a great wall—and nobody builds walls better than me, believe me—and I'll build them very inexpensively. I will build a great, great wall on our southern border, and I will make Mexico pay for that wall.—Donald J. Trump, presidential candidacy announcement, June 16, 2015

Humpty Dumpty sat on a wall
Humpty Dumpty had a great fall. (1797)

Military historians suggest that [China Wall] wasn't especially well-calibrated—to either the contours of its place or the tactics of its times… something conceived and imposed from afar…Over the centuries, people like the Manchus and Mongolians, against whom it was built, found ways through and around.—Thomas de Monchaux, *The New Yorker*, Dec. 11, 2016

A person who thinks only about building walls, wherever they may be, and not building bridges, is not Christian…
—Pope Francis, in-flight news conference, Feb. 18, 2016

The Pope is being used by the Mexican government as a pawn…We're going to stop the drugs coming in and lots of other things…Illegal immigration is killing our country.
—Donald Trump, Fox News, North Charleston, SC,
Feb. 18, 2016

Think Hadrian Wall clarion,
"Guarding against revenant barbarians,
Zombies and other outlanders dicey
George R.R. Martin made it huge and icy.
These great walls are Trumparian.

Trumplandia

For those who want to immigrate,
Trump insists on excessive freight.
Welcoming only very rich
To receive any green card niche.
Everyone else sees the closed gate.

In campaign for democracy,
Trump said he'd fight bureaucracy,
But he offers ugly message
To fans frantic for expressage.
All for building autocracy.

Trump said Judge from Indiana
Couldn't rule on Trump U manna
Because of suspect heritage:
His Mexican parentage.
Trump was holding out for Santa.

Trump scraps sixteen-year tradition:
Cinco de Mayo edition.
But you should really have no fear,
He sent message of his good cheer,
Filled with taco bowl ignition.

Bragged about the guacamole
From the Trump Plaza Grille showy.
Pricey bit with iceberg lettuce.
No sign of rhagoletis.
Claims of "best" are stale baloney.

Tone-deafness with a swelled head.
He's jam-packed with his ego spread,
With no care of how he's received,
Or care of those he might aggrieve.
On M. L. King Day, look for spoon bread.

[H]is shutdown of the government because Congress won't cater to his edifice complex and build a pointless wall.
—Paul Krugman, *New York Times*, Dec. 24, 2018

Trump repeated his false assertion on an imaginary wall 86 times in the seven months before the midterm elections.
—Glenn Kessler, *Washington Post*, Dec. 10, 2018

The criminal aliens who poison our communities with drugs and prey on innocent young people... you've seen the stories about some of these animals…[They'll take a young, beautiful girl, 16, 15 …and they slice them and dice them with a knife because they want them to go through excruciating pain before they die. And these are the animals that we've been protecting for so long.—Donald Trump, speech, Youngstown, Ohio, July 25, 2017

The Trump Organization has secured visas to hire 70 foreign workers who will be employed during the 2017-18 season as maids, cooks, and servers.
—Harriet Sinclair, *Newsweek*, Nov. 5, 2017

Trump said US District Judge Gonzalo Curiel had "an absolute conflict" in presiding over the litigation given that he was "of Mexican heritage" and a member of a Latino lawyers' association…" I'm building a wall. It's an inherent conflict of interest."
 —Brent Kendall, *Wall Street Journal*, June 3, 2016

Trump characterized Judge Curiel as "a hater of Donald Trump, a hater. He's a hater."
 —Nina Totenberg, NPR, June 4, 2016

Happy #CincoDeMayo! The best taco bowls are made in Trump Tower Grill. I love Hispanics!
 —@realDonaldTrump, Twitter, May 5, 2016

This casual Tex-Mex classic seemed out of place in the gilt-laded grill. However, the price matched the over-wrought glitz…the most expensive taco bowl either of us had ever witnessed…with iceberg lettuce.—Kate Taylor & Hollis Johnson, *Business Insider*, May 5, 2017

I get along with everybody…People love me. And you know what? I've been very successful! Everybody loves me.
—Donald J. Trump, CNN Interview, July 8, 2015

Or chitlins on the veranda.
Trump mentions prez of Nambia.
And keeps everyone in their place
So their value he can erase.
Hey! Bring back Carmen Miranda.

After 2010 earthquake,
Thousands of Haitians did emigrate.
Now they're victims of Trump flatus,
Losing Temp Protected Status
While he slurps up his fine milkshake.

Nicaraguans, they are next;
Sudanese in this vile subset.
"Make America Anglo Again!"
Roar from White House playpen.
Norwegians do get his respect.

On values, Trump is worse than vague:
Ignore Haiti's cholera plague.
He is a bully and a punk,
With values aura of a skunk.
Victims need hearing in the Hague.

Puerto Rico without power?
Trump: "Should've worked more hours."
They aren't us,
So Trump feels no fuss.
He demands grovel, not glower.

Trump claims that the Puerto Ricans
Need a stronger workforce beacon.
"They want everything done for them."
He offered paper towels and phlegm.
Texas /Florida not so cheapened.

Code Talkers to be recognized:
But the White House event capsized
By Trump insults so provoking
With his Pocahontas joking.
A narcissist uncivilized.

I'm just beside myself with sadness because our president is a bully, our president is a punk, and he just doesn't get it. I don't know where he was raised but his family didn't do a good job raising that guy.
 —Philadelphia Mayor Jim Kenney on Protected Status decision, NBC, Nov. 2, 2017

Trump Won't Pay a Penny For U.N. Cholera Relief Fund in Haiti.—Headline *Foreign Policy*, June 1, 2017

Two months after Puerto Rico was devastated by Hurricane Maria, a sense of desperation seems to be yielding to resignation at best. More than half of the island is still without power…It has been weeks since President Trump visited to jovially toss rolls of paper towels to needy fellow Americans and brag about how successful the recovery effort was.
 —Editorial, *New York Times*, Nov. 25, 2017

It may be that this company with two employees in small town in Montana was the best choice to rebuild Puerto Rico's electric grid for $300 million in our Tax dollars. But as someone with experience in fighting public corruption in Illinois, this Whitefish Energy deal smells pretty fishy to me.
 —Rep Raja Krisnamoorhi, *The Hill,* Nov. 8, 2017

I think Puerto Rico was incredibly successful…I actually think it was one of the best jobs that's ever been done.
 —Donald Trump from Oval Office, CBS News, Sept. 11, 2018

[At the Navajo Code Talkers] occasion, you can see Trump standing just below a painting of President Andrew Jackson, the architect of the Trail of Tears when 17,000 Native Americans were forced to march from their ancestral homeland in Georgia through freezing temperatures and snow all the way to Oklahoma.
 —Simon Moya-Smith, CNN, Nov. 20, 2017

The Donald has long history
Of words offensive blistery
About Native Americans.
It's not about their pemmican
But his casino rivalry.

Trumpkampf

Now Trump's intent on putting blight
On archeological sites:
Region dense with burial grounds
Ancient rock carvings do abound:
Native American birthright.

Let in Christians, keep Muslims out:
We heard candidate Trump's loud shout.
Now in office, he codifies
This xenophobic ostracize.
Hurling founders vision sellout.

After seven days at his post,
Trump was wholeheartedly engrossed
In banning all Muslim entry.
Assigning border out-sentries
To rebut role as Liberty's host.

Act of contrarianism,
Vicous imperialism,
With airport pandemonium
Nationwide disharmonium.
Reject Trumptarianism!

Islamophobic on Twitter,
Making British PM skitter.
Sarah Sanders, she defended:
Claiming protection front-ended.
Most see ugliness transmitter.

Most definitely not smitten,
Censure came from friends in Britain.
Former Intelligence head says,
This provokes alarm about prez:
If by mad dog he's been bitten.

[The National Indian Gaming Association, a nonprofit group…filed a complaint with the Federal Communications Commission shortly after the 1993 [Trump] interview asking for an investigation into what it called "obscene, indecent and profane racial slurs against Native Americans and African Americans."
—Shawn Boburg, *Washington Post*, July 25, 2016

In an illegal move, the president just reduced the size of Bear and Ears and Grand Staircase Escalante National Monuments. This is the largest elimination of protected land in American history.
—Patagonia homepage.

Patagonia filed a lawsuit in Federal District Court in Washington, naming as defendants Mr. Trump, Interior Secretary Ryan Zinke, the secretary of agriculture, the director of the Bureau of Land Management and the chief of the Forest Service.—December 2017

If you're a Muslim you can come into the country very easy. If you're from Europe and you're a Muslim you can come in. But if you are from Europe and you're a Christian, you can't come in.
—Donald J. Trump, The Brody File, Christian Broadcasting Network, May 20, 2015

[T]oday we still have in our German national body great stocks of Nordic-Germanic people who remain unblended, in whom we may see the most valuable treasure for our future.
—Adolf Hitler, *Mein Kampf* (1925, 20th edition 1999)

For all of President Trump's tweeted thundering about "fake news," one could be forgiven for thinking that he enjoys spreading it himself. What other explanation can there be for Mr. Trump's impulse to retweet three half-baked videos from the website of the UK fringe group Britain First?
—Editorial, *Wall Street Journal*, Dec. 1, 2017

Former Ku Klux Klan leader David Duke praised President Trump…for sharing videos from a far-right British politician purporting to show violence committed by Muslims.
—*The Hill*, Nov. 29, 2017

Receiving praise from David Duke
Would make most people want to puke.
This alumnus Klan Grand Wizard
Is nastier than a gizzard.
But Trump shrugged off others' rebuke.

Trump just cannot identify
With so many immigrants' cries.
Says to hell with all the Dreamers!
He calls them slippery schemers
And all decency nullifies.

But Trump makes Muslim Exception
With his warm Saudi reception—
For cause not meritorious
But profoundly inglorious—
Based on financial conception.

A race-uniform nucleus
Is what Trump finds salubrious.
Would not oppose Hitler salutes
From ugly Charlottesville brown boots.
The hate-spewing Vesuvius.

Ignoring "Don't hug Nazis" rule,
Trump likes to add to the cesspool.
Eager to grab any headline,
He displays the soul of a swine,
Offering prezy papule.

In Charlottesville, came moral rot
With the neo-Nazi buckshot
And touting his local estate
Which hosts all sorts of fancy fetes.
Ever pushing his money pot.

At typical campaign rally,
Trump did offer this fine sally,
With his forked tongue and his tin ear,
"Look at my African American over here!"
Ever in a dark blind alley.

I don't know anything about David Duke, Okay? I don't know anything about what you're even talking about with white supremacy …So I don't know. I mean, I don't know. Did he endorse me? Or what's going on? Because, you know, I know nothing about David Duke.
—Donald Trump, CNN, Feb. 28, 2016

For a normal political, the calculus is simple: Don't hug Nazis.—Matt Taibbi, *Rolling Stone*, Aug. 21, 2017

There must be no further immigration of Non-Germans. The sole exception to this rule has been the incorporation of Czech minorities to occupied areas and the importation of Italian labor.
—Adolf Hitler, *Mein Kampf* (1925, 20th edition 1999)

President Trump has done business with royals from Saudi Arabia for at least 20 years…Mr. Trump has earned millions of dollars from the United Arab Emirates for putting his name on a golf course… "Other countries in the Middle East see what is happening and may think, 'We should be opening golf courses' or 'We should be buying rooms at Trump International,'" said Brian Egan, A State Department legal advisor under the Obama administration.—David D. Kirkpatrick, *New York Times*, June 17, 2017

I've never seen this type of political figure in my life. He's shameless in inspiring violence. He used vile language about people from other countries. He's opened a space for ugliness to come out of the shadows.
—Rabbi Shmuel Herzfeld in Michael Kranish and Marc Fisher, *Trump Revealed: An American Journey of Ambition, Ego, Money, and Power* (2016)

Trump Fascinated By Israeli Cultural Tradition Of Mass Slaughter Of Protesters.
—The Onion, May 14, 2018

I know a lot about Charlottesville. Charlottesville is a great place that's been very badly hurt over the last couple of days. I own, actually one of the largest wineries in the United States. It's in Charlottesville.
—Donald Trump, podium, Trump Tower, Aug. 25, 2017

Jewish Coalition briefing:
Trump offered some ethnic squeezing:
The Kushner "fine Jewish baby."
He plays the crowd without maybes,
Message targets to cloud pleasing.

Trumpickle

For decades, Trump has used the news
To promote his own special schmooze.
Even when showing he's a_ _hole.
Being headliner is the goal.
Top billing is this blighter's booze.

Trump is the model bag of wind.
But first press confab showed thin skin:
Claimed "Biggest crowd in history!"
When fact proved contradictory,
Trump stormed fake news chinny-chin.

Trump always ready with swift kick
To those offering contradict.
Shuns any study of data
To back his unique schemata.
And insists press use his joystick.

Worse than robber baron big shot:
Adds ego to what can be bought.
Enriches his hubris glutton
By pressing those headline buttons,
Uploading dangerous deep rot.

When Fox News sends out the alert,
Zealous fans refuse to divert.
No arguments well-reasoned
With history well-seasoned,
Can sway love for rich stuffed shirt.

For hugs and polity insight,
Trump talks with Hannity each night.
Fox News calls Mueller probe witch hunt,
Advising Trump when he should punt;
White House welcomes troglodytes.

It's impossible to say you're shocked… Bias and bigotry are part and parcel of Trump and his movement. Having a president who is rebuked by world leaders and celebrated by racists has become the new normal.
—Scott Lehigh, *Boston Globe*, Nov. 30, 2017

Our audience isn't going to want me to really ask about Russia or Stormy Daniels. They are just not going to want me to ask.
—David Brody, chief political correspondent, Christian Broadcasting Network to *New York Times*, May 14, 2018

While Mr. Trump attacks major news organizations and suggests revoking media credentials for outlets he deems "Fake News," Mr. Brody and his network enjoy a closeness to the White House that is foreign to most reporters. In return, Mr. Trump gets a direct line to his most supportive voters, the conservative evangelicals who make up CBN's core audience.
—Elizabeth Diaz, *New York Times*, May 14, 2018

Judging from the President's tweets, his definition of "fake news" is credible reporting that he doesn't like. But he complicates the matter by issuing demonstrably false statements of his own, which, inevitably, make news. Trump has brought to the White House bully pulpit a disorienting habit of telling lies, big and small, without evident shame. —Steve Coll, *The New Yorker*, Dec. 11, 2017

We in the commentariat complain about President Trump but he has given us a sense of mission and a "Trump bump." Every time he denounces us we get more subscriptions.—Nicholas Kristof, *New York Times*, May 5, 2018

It is entertainment all the time. The media long ago gave up journalism to keep us amused. Trump was its creation. And now we get a daily "Gong Show" out of the White House. It is good for Trump. It is good for cable news networks' profits. But it is bad for us.
—Chris Hedges, *America: The Farewell Tour* (2018)

[A] flood of managed and fake news so pollutes the flow of information that facts and truth become irrelevant as shapers of public opinion.—Christopher R. Browning, *New York Review of Books,* Oct, 25, 2018

Trump mastered media handling.
Stunts brought front page branding.
Ever a noisy cotillion;
Gave him free ads worth $5 billion,
Media windfall ace landing.

Trumpooze

Here a Black, over there a Jew,
Looking for each opportune cue.
Mostly, no Mexicans are kissed,
But golf club temps on OK list.
Trump employs his verbal doo-doo.

Ask yourself, who's left to shame?
Where will he toss out his next flame?
Little old lady in Des Moines?
Or maybe he'll try Tenderloin?
Always there's someone to defame.

Cut Meals on Wheels to build a wall
And also arts funding recall.
It's regulations atrocious
From mind beset by necrosis.
And more moral touchstones will fall.

Roy Moore to al-Saud connection,
Bundles of values negation.
Trump is at all times cavorting
Amid ethical sell-shorting
With wink to cash genuflection.

Some thought Nambia amusing,
Just a load of mental oozing.
But demarking shithole nations
Does bespeak moral castration,
Causing us all bruising.

It may not be good for America, but it's damn good for CBS... Donald, keep going.—Les Moonves, CBS executive chairman and CEO at Morgan Stanley Technology, Media & Telecom Conference, *Hollywood Reporter*, Feb. 19, 2016

Trump has resumed using his personal cell phone for late-night calls to such confidants as Sean Hannity, of Fox News, who is known in the capital as his "unofficial Chief of Staff."
—Evan Osnos, *The New Yorker,* May 21, 2018

The election proved elite conservative media doesn't matter…Every major non-*Wall Street Journal* columnist was against Trump. *The Weekly Standard* was against Trump. *National Review* was against Trump. None of it mattered… Even as Trump taunts the "failing" *New York Time*s, it's the boutique right-wing media that's truly in peril, now that its lack of influence has been exposed.
—Sam Tannenhaus, *Esquire*, Dec. 20, 2017

The Trump presidency is about Trump. Period. Full stop.
—David Cay Johnston, *It's Even Worse Than You Think: What the Trump Administration Is Doing to America* (2018)

Donald Trump rode $5 billion in free media to the White House.—Headline, The Street, Nov. 20, 2016

The president is at once his own chief of staff, spokesman, national security advisor and top diplomat.
—Richard Haass, President, Council on Foreign Relations, in *Axios*, July 23, 2018

Trump is the most incompetent person to ever become president…Trump is not only insecure and erratic, but uninformed, for he doesn't read history, or know it. Nor does he respect standards of conduct. I expect a real constitutional crisis with Trump…—John Dean, to Seth Hettena, *Rolling Stone*, July 18, 2018

Hail Trump, hail our people, hail victory!—Richard B. Spencer, president, National Policy Institute, "dedicated to the heritage, identity, and future of people of European descent in the U.S. and around the world," Nov. 19, 2016

In racial defenestration,
Trump doesn't speak for our nation,
A place of mix from around the globe.
This missing from Trump's frontal lobe.
As he preaches hate for Haitians.

TV fetish warps whole psyche,
Giving world view Yugely dicey.
One percent of the one percent,
Values encased deep in cement;
Ethos close to *Mein Kampf* icy.

With hubris running frenetic,
Trump sidles up to eugenic.
Says birth gene gives drive for success.
Thankful to be pure Drumpf blessed,
Never mind the frightful fetich.

Kelly: Family bonds are "whatever:"
Children used as ugly lever.
What he defines as deterrence.
We know is shocking occurrence,
Virulent White House dengue fever.

Of course Jeff Sessions did agree
In racial putdown nth degree.
His slimy Beauregard version
Was F-your children perversion;
Fruit from the poisonous Trump tree.

Most saw as moral abscission
Aide's slur on McCain's condition.
But Trump yelled "leakers are traitors!"
Just ammo for Fake News baiters.
No need for White House contrition.

Then there's Cohen selling access
To insider White House bench press.
With a Russinski oligarch
Along with some corporate sharks,
Ponies up for White House noblesse.

A majority of Americans continue to say the United States is a better place to live as a result of its growing racial and ethnic diversity.
—Pew Research Center, June 14, 2018

The Department of Homeland Security says 700 children have been separated from their parents since the fiscal year began last October. —Pete Williams, NBC News, May 7, 2018

[Separating illegal immigrants from children] would be a tough deterrent…The children will be taken care of—put into foster care or whatever.—White House chief of staff John Kelly, NPR, May 11, 2018

Unfortunately, our German nationality is no longer based on a racially uniform nucleus…the blood-poisoning which affected our national body…led not only to a decomposition of our blood but also of our soul…There must be no further immigration of non-Germans.
—Adolf Hitler, *Mein Kampf* (1925, 20th ed. 1999)

If you don't like that, then don't smuggle children over our border.—Attorney General Jeff Sessions, law enforcement conference, Scottsdale, Ariz, May 7, 2018

Only in the Trump Administration would the President's junking of a key nuclear agreement end up as the second-most talked about story of the day…Most observers ending the day chewing over the revelation that Trump's former personal attorney Michael Cohen received half a million dollars last year from a firm associated with a Russian oligarch. The oligarch wasn't the only one paying Cohen.
—John Cassidy, *The New Yorker*, May 9, 2018

Pro golfer Andrew played with The Don
And got a job as whistling swan.
A year later, in 2018,
Dad Rudy joined Trump lawyer team.
Ready with verbal rattle-ons.

To the press Giuliani does bray,
"Trump not involved in any way."
He offers problematic view:
Trump not in on Cohen cash cow.
First time he missed money soiree.

Sessions never did give feedback
On meetings with Sergey Kislak.
Ben Carson considers Putin's
Orthodox creed highfalutin'
Admonishing Muslim blowback.

Zinke, another Putin fanboy,
DeVos' bro back channel convoy;
Pompeo caused lots of tensions
By refusing Senate questions.
No answers for us hoi polloi.

Tillerson's now gone from the gig,
But Jared's there to dance a jig.
Then there was Ruskie money there,
Now there is Ruskie money here,
With jumping on the whirligig.

The staff, they come and they go,
While The People remain in throes.
Chum capitalism's domain
Is the one percenters' gain.
It's time to end this greed road show.

In operation with no heart,
Moving on rapacious flip-charts,
We see evil no longer lurks,
But eagerly sets off fireworks.
Time for Constitution restart.

Giuliani and Vladimar Putin seem to have the same mission here. We have two guys who seem fixated on undermining the credibility of the Department of Justice and the investigation. They seem to be playing from exactly the same playbook.
—Samantha Vinograd, National Security Analyst, CNN, May 28, 2018

Truth isn't truth.—Rudy Giuliani, Meet the Press, Aug. 19, 2018

Ben Carson joined the growing list of American conservatives praising Vladimir Putin'…asserting that Russia is "gaining prestige and influence throughout the world" thanks to Putin's hardline brand of Orthodox Christianity.
—Media Matters for America, Feb. 12, 2014

Presidents are entitled to have private meetings.
—CIA Director Mike Pompeo to Senate Foreign Relations Committee, July 25, 2018

Two years after Donald Trump won the presidency, nearly every organization he has led in the past decade is under investigation.—David A. Fahrenthold, Matt Zapotosky & Seung Min Kim, *Washington Post*, Dec. 15, 2018

[W]e're gonna go in there and we're gonna impeach the motherf*****.— Rep Rashida Tlaib, Jan. 3, 2019

For the country's sake, there is only one acceptable outcome…The president must go.—David Leonhardt, *New York Times*, Jan. 6, 2019

Well, you can't impeach somebody that's doing a great job… I've probably done more in the first two years than any president, any administration, in the history of our country.
—Donald J. Trump, Rose Garden, Jan. 4, 2019

You can be smart, aggressive, articulate, and indeed persuasive. But if you are not honest, your reputation will suffer, and once, lost, a good reputation can never ever be regained.
—Robert Mueller, speaking at his granddaughter's graduation, Tabor Academy, May 29, 2017.

APOCALYPSE

Times have changed.
Any shock we should try to stem
Just results in further mayhem.
Certainly, by now, God knows,
Anything goes.

Presidents who once knew better words
Now drop four-letter words.
And with The Donald's prose,
We all know,
Anything goes.

If mocking Mexicans you like,
If Fox News you like,
If blonde, leggy aides you like,
If border walls you like,
Only Impeachmentists do oppose.
All the Beltway pros know
Anything goes.

If it's ego-maniacs you like,
With their mental loose strife
And moral sell-out you like,
Then admire Melania's clothes
And walk on in a doze.
Just Say No! to impeachment goons
Singing those Loony Tunes.
When you're led by the nose,
Anything goes.

If it's Putin you like,
With insider scandals you like,
And hopes of pee tapes you like,
And money laundering you like,
Just Say No! to the Impeachmentists,
Those Constitutional fundamentalists,
And democracy sentimentalists.

Let go of those frights you've got
And those blights you've got
And that distress you've got
From that fake press you've got.
When The Donald gives you jitters
From abed with his Twitters,
Just recall what The Donald Knows:
Anything goes.

As long as we stand for it:
Anything goes.
Anything goes.

Refuse all cooperation with the
heart's death.
—Mary Oliver, "More Evidence," *Swan* (2010)

POSTSCRIPT: WHY DID THE DONALD CROSS THE ROAD?

A willful beast must go its own way.

—Aesop

It's better to be out than in. It is better to be on the lam than on the cover of Time magazine.

—Nelson Algren

Outside every fat man there's an even fatter man trying to close in.

—Kingsley Amis

To find a piece of cake.

—Marie Antoinette

Panhellenic synergism.

—Aristophanes

It is a sorry business to inquire into what men think, when we are every day
Only too uncomfortably confronted with what they do.

—Michael Arlen

He was in the middle before he knew he had begun.

—Jane Austen

He wanted to go tell it on the mountain.

—James Baldwin

He wanted to get away from the circus for a few minutes.

—P.T. Barnum

To lie drunk
on cobbles
bedded in pinks.

—Basho

To get back to Kansas.

—L. Frank Baum

We are all born mad. Some remain so.

—Samuel Beckett

Daylight come and he wan' go home.
—Harry Belafonte

Late in spring he had been overcome by the need to explain, to have it out, to justify, to put in perspective, to clarify, to make amends.
—Saul Bellow

Everybody has something to conceal.
—Humphrey Bogart/The Maltese Falcon

Donald! Donald! burning bright,
What has caused you to take flight?
—William Blake

Either the road or nothing.
—Caesar Borgia

Above all, turkeys thrive in any movement that focuses on self (self-affirmation, self-realization, self-perpetuation, self-involvement). The appeal of these movements is that they involve no actual change of self.
—Sandra Boynton

To watch the books burn.
—Ray Bradbury

Whether The Donald crossed the road or the road crossed The Donald depends upon your frame of reference.
—Buddha

I never saw a Donald cross the road,
I never hope to see one,
But I'll tell you this,
I'd rather see than be one.
—Galett Burgess

He knew it's time for the human race to enter the solar system.
—George W. Bush

The Donald
relieves his noble bowels
in a desolate field.
      —Buson

It wasn't a road; it was a river.
      —Julius Caesar

To keep America whole and safe and unspoiled.
      —Al Capone

To get down the rabbit hole.
      —Lewis Carroll

He heard that long lonesome whistle blow.
      —Johnny Cash

Finally, from so little sleeping and so much reading, his brain dried up
and he went completely out of his mind.
      —Miguel de Cervantes Savedra

Colorless green ideas sleep furiously.
      —Noam Chomsky

Because he did not have sexual relations with that woman.
      —Bill Clinton

The Donald wished that he, too, had a wound, a red badge of courage.
      —Stephen Crane

To build an iron curtain.
      —Winston Churchill

The Donald believed the White House is primarily a social institution and crossing
the road the fundamental method of social progress and reform.
      —John Dewey

Looking for a far, far better thing to do, than he had ever done.
      —Charles Dickens

Because he could not stop for death.
      —Emily Dickinson

Because the absurd is only too necessary on earth.
      —Fyodor Dostoyevsky

How often have I said to you that when you have eliminated the impossible, whatever remains, *however improbable*, must be the truth?
—Arthur Conan Doyle

He dreamt he was walkin' into World War Three.
—Bob Dylan

He wasn't doing it because he wanted to take long showers with assholes.
—Clint Eastwood

To check the parallel transport of vectors.
—Albert Einstein

Some men get the world, some men get ex-hookers and a trip to Arizona.
—James Ellroy

We cast a shadow on something wherever we stand, and it is no good moving from place to place to save things; because the shadow always follows.
—E. M. Forster

Sometimes a road is just a road.
—Sigmund Freud.

The Donald didn't want to live an unlived life.
—Erich Fromm

Because that road was the one most traveled.
—Robert Frost

He was privileged to be invited to a family festival of capitalists, a one-percent family in full plumage.
—John Galsworthy

Looking for the enemy of the people.
— Joseph Goebbels

To go messing about in boats.
—Kenneth Grahame

To take a basket of fruit to his grandmother.
—Grimm brothers

He was a hurricane of entitlement, all swirl and noise and destruction, nothing at his center.
—Lauren Groff

He'd heard you can get anything you want at Alice's Restaurant.
—Arlo Guthrie

A dead iguana fell from a palm tree and hit him on the head.
—Carl Hiassen

It wasn't a road; it was a mountain.
—Hannibal

What we have to remember is that what we observed is not Trump in himself but Trump exposed to our method of questioning.
—Werner Heisenberg

Because he was the master of his fate and the captain of his soul.
—W. E. Henley

Lebensraum.
—Adolph Hitler

To see some very interesting conditioning for Alpha Plus Intellectuals.
—Aldous Huxley

Cause "The Nigga he love to hate" still can "Kill at Will."
—Ice Cube

A man may build himself a throne of bayonets, but he can't sit on it.
—William Ralph Inge

It is not the answer that enlightens, but the question.
—Eugene Ionesco

Looking for a place to take a nap.
—Washington Irving

'Cause it's lonely lonely lonely at the top.
—Mick Jagger

He worried about that little rebellion, now and then, being a good thing and as necessary in the political world as storms in the physical.
—Thomas Jefferson

He wanted to join me and march along the road to the future, the road that leads to the Great Society, where no child will go unfed and no youngster will go unschooled.
—Lyndon Johnson

An irrepresentable, unconscious, pre-existent form seemed to be part of The Donald's inherited structure and could manifest itself in spontaneous crossing anywhere, at any time.
—Carl Jung

Someone must have been telling lies about The Donald.
—Franz Kafka

That's where the railroad tracks were.
—Anna Karenina
He didn't.
Crossed roads are sweet, but those uncrossed
Are sweeter.
—John Keats

He wanted to be on the road.
—Jack Kerouac

Some things it don't pay to be curious about.
—Stephen King

He's looking for where all the flowers have gone.
—Kingston Trio

If you build it, The Donald will come to put his name on it.
—William Kinsella

The Donald takes his fun where he finds it.
—Rudyard Kipling

In search of sexual perversion.
—Baron Richard Von Krafft-Ebing

As a committed anarchist, The Donald jaywalked because the rules of the state are the chief instrument for permitting the few to monopolize the land.
—Prince Peter Alekseyevich Kropotkin

The Donald, cut off from his own mind, cut off equally from his own body—
a half-crazed creature in a mad world.
—R. D. Laing

A journey of a thousand miles must begin with a single step across the road.
—Lao-Tsu

The Donald believed his gut is wiser than intellect.
—D. H. Lawrence

Because he wanted to get away from the huddled masses.
—Emma Lazarus

To sit quietly and smell the flowers.
—Munro Leaf

It wasn't a road; it was an ocean.
—Charles Lindbergh

It is the right of every Donald to cross the road.
—James Madison

Power never takes a back step.
—Malcolm X

Our principle is that the Party commands The Donald, and The Donald must never be allowed to cross the road.
—Chairman Mao

Because the government had fooled him into thinking that he was crossing the road of his own free will, when he was really only serving their interests.
—Karl Marx

He was dancing, dancing. He says he'll never die.
—Cormac McCarthy

Looking for illegal aliens.
—Joseph McCarthy

It wasn't to make way for ducklings.
—Robert McCloskey

Innumerable confusions and a feeling of despair invariably emerge in periods of great technological and cultural transition.
    —Marshall McLuhan

Because he didn't know it's better to cross with a drunken reporter than a sober Republican.
    —Herman Melville

Unrest of spirit is a mark of life.
    —Karl Menninger

He hadn't learned the truth that men make terrible pigs.
    —Madeline Miller

It was better than sitting in darkness, hatching vain empires.
    —John Milton

He thought he was in the land of cotton. Hoorah! Hoorah!
    —Bryant's Minstrels

That's where the money is.
    —J. P. Morgan

Because he was a body in motion.
    —Isaac Newton.

It's hard to be free when you're bought and sold in the market place
    —Jack Nicholson/Easy Rider

There are no facts, only interpretations.
    —Friedrich Nietzsche

To begin a long day's journey into night.
    —Eugene O'Neill

All are equal to cross but some are more equal than others,
    —George Orwell

In a hierarchy every president tends to rise to his level of road-crossing incompetence.
    —Peter Principle

It was developmentally appropriate for The Donald to do so.
—Jean Piaget

Surely The Donald walketh in a vain show.
—Psalm 39:6

Looking for a fight. The Donald loves the sting of battle.
—General George Patton

He wanted to get out of the Cave.
—Plato

You can't stay in your corner of the Forest waiting for others to come to you. You have to go to them sometimes.
—Winnie the Pooh

The Family made The Donald an offer he couldn't refuse.
—Mario Puzo

He needed to get out of nature and go worship skyscrapers.
—Ayn Rand

He didn't want to be sittin' on the dock of the bay.
—Otis Redding

Crossing the road was the last taboo of Trumpdom.
—Theodor Reik

To extend his rule throughout the world.
—Cecil Rhodes

The way to make money is to buy when blood is running in the streets.
—John D. Rockefeller

He failed to win one for the Gipper.
—Knute Rockne

To go boldly where no man has gone before.
—Gene Roddenberry, Star Trek

Because he wanted to avoid any New Deal.
—Franklin Delano Roosevelt

It wasn't a road; it was a hill.
      —Theodore Roosevelt

He was the Raskolnikov of jerking off.
      —Philip Roth

Looking for sex.
      —Dr. Ruth

It was too early to sing and dance at funerals.
      —Carl Sandburg

Because he was a fanatic, he forgot why he wanted to cross the road.
      —George Santayana

The Donald understood that he must count on no one but himself, that he is alone, sbandoned on earth in the midst of infinite responsibilities, without help, with no other aim than the one he sets himself.
      —John Paul Sartre

It wasn't a road; it was a tunnel.
He climbed through darkness to the twilight air,
Unloading hell behind him step by step.
      —Siegfried Sassoon

Life swings like a pendulum backward and forward between pain and boredom.
      —Arthur Schopenhauer

I don't feel like going into it, if you want to know the truth.
      —J. D. Salinger

It's where the wild things are.
      —Maurice Sendak

He's on his own
And you know what he knows.
And HE is the one who'll decide where to go...
      —Dr. Seuss

You would pluck out the heart of my mystery.
      —William Shakespeare

When a stupid is doing something he is ashamed of, he always declares that it is his duty.
      —George Bernard Shaw

It's where the sidewalk ends.
        —Shel Silverstein

It wasn't a road; it was a bridge…over troubled water.
       —Simon & Garfunkel

The light changed; The Donald walked.
        —B. F. Skinner

Go ask Alice.
        —Grace Slick

Every man, as long as he does not violate the laws of justice, is left perfectly free to pursue his own interest his own way, and to bring both his industry and capital into competition with those of any other man.
        —Adam Smith

You can't make a revolution without crossing the road.
        —Joseph Stalin
It wasn't a road; it was a railroad track.
        —Leland Stanford

There ain't no answer. There ain't going to be any answer. There never has been an answer. That's the answer.
        —Gertrude Stein
Among twenty Republicans
The only puzzling one
Was The Donald who crossed the road.
        —Wallace Stevens
Cannon to right of him,
Cannon to left of him,
Cannon behind him.
        —Alfred Lord Tennyson

He who commands the road has command of everything.
        —Thermistocles

He did not want to go gentle into that good night.
        —Dylan Thomas

He didn't. The Donald stops here.
        —Harry Truman

I had the story, bit by bit, from various people, and, as generally happens in such cases, each time it was a different story.
—Edith Wharton

He had too much time on his hands.
—Thorstein Veblen

It is a great misfortune to be alone… and it must be believed that solitude can quickly destroy reason.
—Jules Verne

We are not interested in The Donald
—Queen Victoria

The Donald is free the moment he wants to be.
—Voltaire

Listen: The Donald has come unstuck in time.
—Kurt Vonnegut

To celebrate himself.
—Walt Whitman

He didn't know the precise psychological moment when to do nothing.
—Oscar Wilde

So much depends
upon The Donald
seeing a road
and a path between the
white lines.
—William Carlos Williams

He couldn't go home again.
—Thomas Wolfe

He was looking for the way to Byzantium—or Moscow.
—William Butler Yeats

Without deviation, progress is not possible.
—Frank Zappa

www.ingramcontent.com/pod-product-compliance
Lightning Source LLC
Chambersburg PA
CBHW080026130526
44591CB00037B/2689